DROWNING IN TIMIDITY

WOMEN, POLITENESS & THE POWER OF ASSERTIVE LIVING

Cara Tuttle Bell

Drowning in Timidity

Copyright © 2021 by Cara Tuttle Bell

All rights reserved.

Publisher:
Cara Tuttle Bell

Publishing Consultant:
Professional Woman Publishing
www.pwnbooks.com

ISBN: 978-0-578-24970-4

For Raelin.

To Chelsea, Candace, Sarah, Danielle, Becca,
Asheeka, Kait, Siri, Andrew, Mahek, Regan, Brionna,
and for all the dear students from my years
at JCC, USC Upstate, Northwestern, and Vanderbilt
who make tough work worth doing.

To Kenneth "Butch" Avery Tuttle, my father,
who always delighted in my feisty nature
and determination and modeled both.

Contents

Introduction ix

Chapter 1	The Politeness Trap	1
Chapter 2	Who You Are and Who You Want to Be	9
Chapter 3	The Work of Undoing	21
Chapter 4	The Work of Doing: Get in There!	31
Chapter 5	Guarding Against Taking the Easy Way Out (or Assertiveness as Allyship)	41
Chapter 6	Embracing Fear, Insecurity, and Uncertainty	55
Chapter 7	Your Personal Relationship Rights	67
Chapter 8	Assertiveness at Work	79
Chapter 9	Raise Hell and Raise Angry Girls	91
Chapter 10	Collective Assertiveness and Responsibility	101

Acknowledgments 107

Notes 109

About the Author 113

Introduction

I am living the life I've always wanted. You can, too. If you already know this, wonderful, and welcome! If you have doubts yet want this to be true, keep reading. Today, my life is a satisfying, well-rounded, and primarily my own creation, although I was not always assertive in advocating for myself, or for others. That is how I know with certainty that assertiveness is a skill that can be learned, regardless of how we were raised. Some of you may be starting at the beginning. Some of you may feel confident in some areas of your life but not others. Very few of us received any sort of assertiveness training at any point along the way, although almost without exception, we were taught politeness. And while I believe in extending politeness to others and believe in the importance of good manners, I don't believe in the gendered socialization of politeness as silence, passivity, and self-sacrifice to an extent that denies to some of us the ability to boldly create and live authentic, creative, satisfying, safe, healthy, and productive lives.

Within this book are steps which you may take to further your journey away from timidity toward assertive living. Assertiveness is the muscle we must build and then flex, as needed. Assertiveness is the method of advocating for self while still valuing and respecting others. Your good manners may come along for this ride. In fact, you will need that internal gauge to help you identify the parts of yourself that too easily come on strong or too hastily seek retreat. When assertiveness is confused with aggressiveness, our inner selves may feel inadequate or out of whack. Since assertiveness has at its core a sense of balance

– balancing the needs or wants of self in relation to others – assertiveness training may help us feel a more regular sense of balance in our lives. This balance can help bring about more egalitarian relationships, and don't we all want better, stronger, healthier relationships?

People in this nation and in many parts of the world are angry, divided, anxious, and depressed. Many feel disempowered and disillusioned by aspects of the world around them. While assertiveness alone isn't necessarily the cure-all and a single act of assertiveness may not significantly shift these dynamics, I know for certain that assertiveness can change our lives, and, cumulatively, collectively, we can change the world.

This book starts with you. In my typical fashion, you will get a pep talk, some homework, and occasional tough love. You may experience doubt and discomfort, but push through – that's how growth occurs. You may find that the usefulness of exercising assertiveness on your own behalf soon extends to family and friends and then to the world around you. Assertive women are my greatest cheerleaders, my occasional safety net, and my closest friends. They bolster my self-confidence, self-respect, and self-worth. Through these mutually affirming relationships, I have come to believe assertiveness training holds the power to ultimately build the sisterhood and solidarity many of us have always wanted. We are so ready to welcome you to join us today.

CHAPTER ONE

The Politeness Trap

"Politeness is fictitious benevolence."

— Samuel Johnson —

Politeness is generally considered useful, appropriate behavior. Sure. And I hope for the most part, you engage with other humans with consideration and respect. Yet I do not want us to retreat into politeness when our courage is waning or use expectations of politeness as an excuse to hold ourselves back. If you consider the definition of the word "politeness," you may be surprised at how similar the definition is to how we are applying assertiveness here. Whether you consult Merriam-Webster or Dictionary.com, the definitions explain politeness as engaging with courtesy, tact, consideration, and respect.[1] Because there is a difference in engaging assertively and aggressively, you can absolutely be both assertive and polite at the same time. A few dated definitions of politeness do include deference among its characteristics, and for women, especially, the challenge may be in learning how to use that deference sparingly and strategically.

Women remain subject to gendered societal expectations, while we've also internalized messages about equity, equality, and advancement that now span generations. This complicated status quo means that many a woman develops career aspirations and knows she is expected to engage in competitive American work cultures, and so works to build confidence engaging in public speaking, salary negotiation, raising her hand, leaning forward, leaning in. And yet our progress seems slow – slower than expected and with less joy and less money along the way. Many women come to believe this is an individual problem – they didn't work hard enough, they don't have what it takes – when actually we're all very much still navigating the growing pains of women's full participation in the workforce, while also struggling to get our efforts to value diversity and build cultures of inclusion and belonging in our schools, professions, and communities for anyone who isn't white, heterosexual, cisgender, able-bodied, and male.

Many assertiveness guides focus solely on the individual, and here, too, the bulk of the work will focus on who and what we can control, and that is usually just ourselves. In each chapter you find individual exercises designed to build your own confidence and assertiveness skills, prompting growth which is intended to come with the responsibility to also use on behalf of others. This dual approach is just part of what it will take to actually create much-needed, long overdue change and reach those espoused values of inclusion and belonging, for all of us. So, while women remain subject to discrimination, women also are responsible, at times, for its perpetration and perpetuation.

Women report experiencing more incivility at work than do men, although it is important to note that not all of that incivility is due to sexism. It is not all inflicted by men; plenty of the incivility is conducted by women against women.[2] While there are many aspects of gendered socialization that may play out in the workplace, particularly in currently and historically male-dominated professions, sometimes we need to deploy assertiveness in our interactions with and among women. Other times, however, we must stop and look at ourselves

— are we the problem? Are we judging women for engaging assertively at work? Research suggests we are.

A 2018 study by researchers Allison S. Gabriel, Marcus M. Butts, and Michael T. Sliter found that "when women acted more assertively at work — expressing opinions in meetings, assigning people to tasks, and taking charge — they were even more likely to report receiving uncivil treatment from other women at work. We suspect that it may be that women acting assertively contradicts the norms that women must be warm and nurturing rather than emphatic and dominant. This means that women who take charge at work may suffer backlash in the form of being interpersonally mistreated."[3] Sadly, assertive women may still be viewed as some sort of threat by other women. Personal insecurity and notions of scarcity (i.e., there's only room for so many women) make women view other women with distrust and as competition. So, it seems that we do not always lift as we climb.

While messages of women's empowerment and solidarity permeate social media and are now widely available on all manner of products available for purchase (shirts, keychains, stickers, travel mugs, cross-stitch and embroidery kits, you name it), I am wondering how many workplace "girl tribes" actually exist and how many #womensupportingwomen hashtags are added to posts by women who are, perhaps, better at sisterhood in theory than in practice. When acts of solidarity count the most, we're too often found lacking.

> "An assumption underlying almost all comments on interruptions is that they are aggressive, but the line between what's perceived as assertiveness or aggressiveness almost certainly shifts with an interrupter's gender."
>
> **DEBORAH TANNEN**

Women typically hold less individualistic beliefs and values, yet these lingering expectations of politeness, particularly gendered notions of politeness, get in the way of women being effective intervening bystanders when they witness incivility, harassment, discrimination, and violence, whether in the home, the community, or the workplace. The politeness trap isn't merely holding you back – the politeness trap can make us complicit in racism, sexism, homophobia, ethnocentrism, transphobia, misogyny, ableism, xenophobia, and other serious harms. There is no neutral. When you do nothing, you are allowing that violence and discrimination to exist in and therefore be the world as we know it. Your inaction emboldens the bad behavior and sends the message to the target of that discrimination that you do not care enough to do anything about what they have experienced. Particularly when we consider white women who do not speak out against white supremacy, the politeness trap is no excuse. Your refusal to acknowledge what is going on in your country, your refusal to engage in politics or discuss serious matters publicly, is only possible due to privilege, coupled with conflict avoidance. Your silence proves the existence of your privilege. Those who do not hold the same privilege cannot risk staying silent – their lives literally depend upon it. If reading these words hits too close to home for you, if you're considering putting this book away because it isn't simply offering you the excuses or pep talks you were seeking, please know that this isn't meant as judgmental scolding. This is a call to action. This already offers one of those promised moments for growth. You can survive a difference of opinion and a little cognitive dissonance. You can change your perspective and your self-awareness and your behavior today. Living with clarity and authenticity, living assertively, means confronting harsh realities self-reflexively – looking directly at what is happening and asking why, and what can I do about it? Lingering sexism also means women can hold themselves to lower expectations, but I hope you avoid that cowardice. Let's hold on tightly right now to those high expectations that prompted you to buy this book. Moments of uncertainty and disagreement should feel possible. After all, those are unavoidable parts of the human experience. This discussion is merely calling you to be active and engaged in your own life and community. If white women can protest and organize to ensure their children get to experience prom and graduation, as we have witnessed mothers do *despite pandemic restrictions*, we can get out and support Black mothers who are desperately and painfully asking us to care about their children being murdered far too frequently, including by those who are supposed to offer protection to us all. Living assertively means confronting our inner contradictions and facing our fears and advocating for *both* ourselves and others. We cannot continue to focus solely on individual acts of self-improvement when the world is in turmoil all around us. Some women are drowning in timidity, while the world burns.

You do not want to be one of those women, those people, or you would not be here. Self-reflection is crucial; you cannot successfully use assertiveness if you do not know yourself. While there are times we may be able to convincingly "fake it 'til you make it," you should avoid convincing yourself that such a patchwork approach will take you as far as you want to go. Take the next few minutes to explore how you are feeling about the challenge posed to you here. Use the exercises on the next few page to begin pulling your thoughts and feelings outside of you, so that they are no longer cautiously or fearfully hidden within, and let's get to work.

> "You don't knock another sister, ever. There's room for everybody on this planet; you don't have to be like anyone else."
>
> **CYNDI LAUPER**

DROWNING IN TIMIDITY

DATE

ASSERTIVENESS SELF CHECK-IN
Consider your responses to the following questions.

If someone used the word "assertive" to describe me, I would feel:

My assertive human role models are:

I chose them because...

My short-term assertiveness building goals are:

My long-term assertiveness building goals are:

THE POLITENESS TRAP

ASSERTIVE DOODLING
SCRATCH PAPER

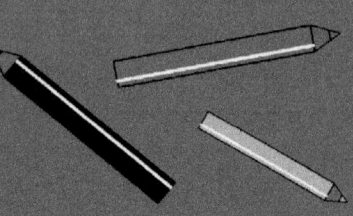

How are you feeling right now in this moment? Without overthinking -- sincerely -- scratch out any visual representation of your feelings in the space below. Get them out! All feelings are valid. No self-censoring in this exercise. Talent not required.

CHAPTER TWO

Who You Are and Who You Want to Be

> *"Doubt can motivate you, so don't be afraid of it. Confidence and doubt are at two ends of the scale, and you need both. They balance each other out."*
>
> — Barbra Streisand —

How do you describe yourself? When I ask you, "Who are you?" what words come first to mind? Try to describe yourself with three descriptive phrases right now, as we begin this second chapter. For so many women, the word "just" shows up in the answer, even when the question itself is so limiting! Did you say to yourself, "I'm just a mom," or "I'm just a program coordinator," "just a college student," or "just a nurse" or "just a teacher"? Why "just"? Is that work not trying, tiring, and satisfying? Look around. Consider your colleagues. Does it appear that everyone is equally good at what you do?

The word "just" is a qualifier. It is used to diminish or limit, in some way, whatever comes next. It is often an unnecessary word, one that could easily be removed from most sentences and yet the sentences still get the job done. Who uses the word "just" more frequently? Women, of course, along with anyone whose identity is linked to a disproportionate lack of privilege and belonging, which often contributes to imposter syndrome or other lack of confidence.

The word "just" is also often used to resist accountability. It's still a qualifier, sure, but one routinely used by those who are not living fully, authentically…you guessed it – assertively. Many women employ the word "just" in this way, as an excuse for their own unhealthy, intrusive, controlling, judgmental beliefs and actions. "Just" is used to cover a multitude of sins, conveniently relied upon by those who choose to sit in immaturity, who may never step into assertiveness, opting instead to avoid taking responsibility for their thinking, their choices, their weaknesses and inaction.

This type of woman can cause serious damage. Generationally, and historically, this practice makes some sense – when and where equality has been denied, the more we often find these forms of indirect power-seeking and intragroup control fester. For many, choosing to conform and live (they imagine) safely is only comfortable if they can get you, too, to live that way. Change is fraught with risk. As is growth. As is responsibility. The assertive person takes action and moves forward. The unassertive person chooses to remain still. Stillness is valuable in its place and time; however, when still becomes stuck, we have a problem.

You know the type – she offers her opinion, some comment about how someone other than herself should be doing something differently, and then follows up with the throw-away statement, "I'm just a _____ (sub your pal's proudest self-given label here). Let's use "I'm just a mom" as an example. I hear that all the time. The shrug of the shoulders, paired with the word "just" here is meant to imply a lack of responsibility for the pressure or control she is trying to exert, contains within itself a denial of accountability for the inappropriateness or hypocrisy of the claim she is making, and is designed to minimize blowback from others who may disagree with her or resist this type of passive-aggressive social policing. Then, when someone disagrees, the "just" can be repositioned and repurposed, yet again, in further deflection through faux self-deprecation, shapeshifting to now take the tone of, "but what do I know?" I've seen this wielded masterfully, sure. (Mothers and mothers-in-law both real and on-screen come to mind.) For all the good intentions that may accompany this practice, the method leaves much to be desired. This communication style remains indirect and unaccountable. Masked manipulation often comes out as "mean girl" behavior. This undermines trust and connection. This reinforces stereotypes about women and our rumored limitations, whereas living assertively means avoiding undermining yourself and weakening your own position.

Let's explore a specific example. Mothers (related to us or not) routinely ask childless women when they are going to have children. When, not if. And worse, what follows – the why or why not? My question is this, though: Why do they get to ask (to pry – let's call it what it is)? If any resistance to this questioning is conveyed, then comes the shrug, and probably the comment, "I'm just a mom." PSA, friends – Stop asking everyone this question. As singles and couples struggle with infertility and miscarriages, illness and disease, you do not need to interrupt someone's day, especially when you do not know them very well, to bring up this very private decision or journey, *just* because you have made the same or a different choice. You do not need to impose your choice onto others. Whether women lean in or opt out, whether they choose to navigate the world as a woman in the same way you might have, what does that take away from you? Why is it your business? You probably don't intend to care for the children of the stranger you are asking. We have a culture of women obsessed with the potential motherhood of others, yet we have thousands of children in foster care, thousands hungry, and thousands housed in detention centers in this country alone. Nah, ladies. No, thank you. I don't buy it.

This is not an attack on motherhood. Motherhood is incredibly tough and deserves its reverence. Mothers and grandmothers and aunts and sisters – they are all so often amazing. The amount of sacrificial, unpaid labor they provide IS amazing. And this need not be a gendered, unpaid obligation to remain appreciated. Motherhood need not *require* as much sacrifice – even though you yourself might choose to make that sacrifice time and time again. I regularly assertively champion the recognition of these contributions and sacrifices and advocate for our government and workplaces to truly embrace the family values they put so much warm rhetoric behind. Few childless women would argue that remote work, extended parental leave, work hour flexibility, and other "family-friendly" policies should not be in place. In fact, they often welcome these practices and policies. Childless women are not your enemy. So-called "career women" are not your enemy. Trust me, career women know motherhood is hard work! It is difficult enough to be a "career woman," children or not. It is difficult enough to be a working parent, woman or not. Yet we have a vocal subset of women who continue championing "traditional" values, who talk about women "trying to have it all," and who claim selflessness while shaming other women. But if you chose to have children and that was both a desire and a choice you made freely, how is that selfless? Plenty of women admit to pressuring their partners to have more children than their partners say they want. Mothers and mothers-in-law are often freely willing to offer their tips on how to convince (or trick) a husband (even their own sons!) into having that next child. How is that selfless and not selfish? How is that service? For many, that's the life of your dreams and design, the life you always wanted. Why does it also need to be a life you impose upon others? Why even the pressure? I find this mind-boggling.

The "just" women uphold the patriarchy by policing gender while faking self-deprecation. Career women are doing gender wrong, they believe. Many career women make up the teams of caregivers providing a service to their children 24-hours a day, mind you. They may be nannies, daycare workers, social workers, counselors, victim advocates, lawyers, teachers, nurses, school staff, doctors, police officers, and on and on and on. Many career women with children feel bad about the time work takes them from their children, and many career women work with such dedication that they delay or forego having children of their own because they take care of yours.

> **patriarchy**
> /ˈpātrēˌärkē/
> noun
> - a system of society or government in which the father or eldest male is head of the family and descent is traced through the male line.
> - a system of society or government in which men hold the power and women are largely excluded from it.
> - a society or community organized on patriarchal lines.
> plural noun: patriarchies
> Example: "we live in a patriarchy"
>
> **OXFORD ENGLISH DICTIONARY**

Consider the whole team of other women in your community that take care of you, your friends and family, of youth or elders. Women also do the most volunteering, of course, too. Work of human and community value that is necessary but typically unpaid, in true American capitalist fashion. And there are women themselves that don't value this work! Not as *work*, anyway. Despite the large numbers of humans that need such care, and despite how essential this work is to the smooth functioning of our society. Many, many women provide work that provides a much-needed service, while being labeled selfish. But with hundreds of thousands of children in the U.S. in the foster care system, and with judgmental women abound not answering that call, something about this line of thinking comes up empty. Because often the pressure that some women pose on other women is not pressure to adopt, not to foster, but to birth your own children and focus so intensely on their raising that jobs, but not a career, is possible. Now, humankind as a species is not at risk of going extinct. Not due to career women's choices, at any rate. So, what is this judgment really about? Is this truly about the children, or is it wanting other women to "do" gender the same way you do? And here I thought independence was a treasured American value. You know, our "independent spirit," and "American independence." What do we even mean by "American independence"? Who does that apply to? Who gets to be independent?

Why, or why not?

Consider independence in the context of the motherhood discussion. If you already understand the term "reproductive freedom," chances are you already understand how assertiveness is linked to independence, and how insecurity can be linked to conformity. We must embrace independence if we are going to authentically develop assertiveness. Otherwise, we're just faking assertiveness from time to time, while probably giving assertiveness a bad name. Let's compare and contrast the independent person to the insecure person. Who caves to social pressure? Who needs others to live the way they do? Who tolerates difference? Who champions diversity? Who moves forward with compassion for others? Who engages civically with respect for others?

If I understand myself to be a fully formed independent adult human, why would I need those outside of the walls of my home to live in accordance with my tastes and preferences? Let's work through another example because while assertiveness is useful to those of all gender identities, our understanding of assertiveness remains so wrapped up in existing gender stereotypes that more than a few of us may benefit from some time spent unpacking the mess. The pockets of the population holding tightly onto dated gender norms are holding us back. This is not merely annoying. These policewomen of gender norms, with their assumption that people are doing gender wrong, police gender all day long, with serious consequences. If I understand myself to be a fully formed, independent adult, why would I need to know, just by looking, someone's gender? Overwhelmingly, the gender identity of another does not make or break my day. Their genitalia? Almost NEVER relevant. While there may be limited circumstances in which gender actually matters, it's actually far more likely that we're projecting some wildly exaggerated importance to gender in our daily lives. Doubt me? Reflect on this for one day. If I stop at a gas station to get gas on my way to work, in the light of day, with others just going about their business, do I need to recognize or confirm the gender of any other stranger around me? Probably not.

If I am speeding in my car on my way to work and get pulled over by a police officer, is there any reason that I would need to understand and label the officer's gender, as they approach the car and interact with me? Probably not. If I arrive at work, having had my morning coffee, and realize that I need to use the restroom, what reason would I have to label the gender of every person I pass along the way to the restroom? None. I know my own gender, and I make my own choice as to which restroom I use (that's both an independent action and a reflection of my privilege). I've got to tell you, as we've arrived to the toilet in this scenario, that the gender of a person next to me in a stall divided by a wall and door matters not. And let me add, the gender of the person in that stall before me, matters not. We all routinely use restrooms frequented by people of all genders, by those who look like us and those who don't. Frankly, when I have to use the bathroom, I choose not to get in my own way.

Now, some of you may not know why we have arrived here or where this conversation between us is going. Let me state it plainly – sometimes living assertively means minding our own business. Return to the definition of assertiveness. Assertiveness is the method of advocating for self while still valuing others. Instead of "my way or the highway" (essentially a dictatorship with a false choice to opt out), assertive living sometimes means, quite simply, you get to use the restroom and you let others use it, too. When we consider assertiveness as something separate from entitlement, force, majority rule, and steamrolling, we can harness the power of assertiveness for collective action and improvement. Some of you are still trying to be benevolent dictators, ruling over your friends, families, clubs and associations, churches and workplaces, from your seat of limited power. Surely compassion means we do not stop others from using the restroom safely and as needed. Surely independent thinking means I do not need other people to choose the same car, the same vacation spot, the same clothing, the same hobbies, the same school districts, the same, the same, the same. If you cannot browse social media without finding comparison to be the thief of joy, without feeling judgmental or insecure, or finding yourself pulled into low-stakes and manufactured controversies, there's more work to do. Minding your own business is easy when you like your own life. Does this feel out of reach?

If you picked up this book in hopes of building skills to advance your own self-interest in selfish ways, you may be feeling disappointed or lost right now. That is okay. Right now, we are unlearning. Continue on. Many of the skills you can build may be used for harm or good. You may need to get newly comfortable with the word "selfish." The word is wielded against women, especially certain types of women. And worse, the word is used by some women (often those who heavily embrace the passive-aggressive approach) against other women. But what's so wrong with some selfishness from time to time? Is the only path for women a life of sacrifice and putting others first? Is selfishness wrong if it doesn't harm others? Do the women you know who do that or claim to do that seem happy, healthy, and satisfied? Even if on the purported path of selflessness, might they be harming others with their depression, dissatisfaction, and resentment? Balance is not selfish. Self-care is not selfish. "Me time" is healthy and has regenerative effects. Sleep is not selfish. Is any of this actually even selfishness? I reject the premise. Women need to move away from this conceptualization altogether and recognize that service takes many forms that are both personally and socially meaningful. We need to pause to take stock of how much of ourselves we are giving to others, *why*, and how much of that giving is getting us where we want and need to be.

Assertive living advances your cause, your health and wellbeing, your family, your community while considering and, hopefully, respecting the rights, wants, and needs of others. When we fail to grasp this, we are often playing into sexist, patriarchal thinking. When we criticize other women for their conformity or lack thereof to our own ideals of womanhood, we may be perpetuating gender-based inequality. Assertiveness and ambition are not dirty words. Both can help us better care for our friends and our families, not just ourselves.

On the next three pages, you will find exercises designed to help you self-reflect. We must acknowledge who we are and we must be willing to learn from our past behavior, particularly to identify patterns of behavior, if we are able to create change and move forward toward becoming who we want to be.

PATTERNS AND SOLUTIONS

REVIEWING PAST CHALLENGES

Consider 3 times in your life when you did not achieve something that you wanted. These previous experiences may be personal or professional. Briefly describe the situation and consider internal and external factors that may have contributed to this setback. Remember, we all experience failure, and we can all learn from it.

_____
_____
_____
_____
_____
_____
_____
_____
_____
_____
_____
_____

INTERROGATING SELFISHNESS

Complete the writing prompts below in numerical order.

1. Excluding family members, list people you know who you consider selfish.

2. What makes them selfish?

3. What possible explanations other than selfishness might explain their behavior?

4. If these people were of another gender, would you judge their behavior the same way?

5. How might these people describe you? In what ways might people think you are being selfish? What would you want them to know?

PATTERNS AND SOLUTIONS

REVIEWING PAST CHALLENGES

Consider the three experiences you identified earlier. Now, as if you were an outside observer or judge, identify key facts — not feelings — linked to the situation. What do you know, if you're being self-reflexive, about the progression of events? Did you communicate your wants and needs assertively at that time? If not, why?

HISTORICAL FACTS	CRITICAL ANALYSIS
HISTORICAL FACTS	CRITICAL ANALYSIS

CONCLUSION

CHAPTER THREE

The Work of Undoing

"Women have to be active listeners and interrupters — but when you interrupt, you have to know what you are talking about."

— Madeleine Albright —

It is okay to say no. It is okay to quit something. It is okay to disagree with someone. It is okay to complicate a plan or decision. It really is. You may have read this in women's magazines or business or self-help non-fiction books, and I hope so. I hope this feels repetitive. Redundant. Because for many women, getting to a place of acceptance of the *no* and the difficulty bears repeating this message. There is ample evidence of gender differences in socialization, and there are also personality differences, birth order in various family sizes, experiences of tragedy or abuse, and other life events and factors that may result in women, in particular, struggling to engage in the world assertively. Those forces that have shaped us are valid, but not necessarily useful. Perhaps they served us at one time but, alas, no longer. So you might find it useful to begin building assertiveness skills by engaging in the work of undoing. Let's identify and abandon those tendencies that are holding us back. Let's learn the power of an unexplained "no" and the benefits of a good quit every now and then. If you've been pleasantly going along in life for this long, you've definitely earned the break.

Granted, sometimes assertiveness means doing the thing, honoring the commitment. Life tells us, though, well, it depends. As Mary Laura Philpott, author of *I Miss You When I Blink* (and an Emmy-winning co-host of A Word on Words, the lively literary mini-program on Nashville Public Television) writes, "[M]aybe the trick isn't sticking everything out. The trick is quitting the right thing at the right time. The trick is understanding that saying, 'No, thank you' to something you're expected to accept isn't failure. It's a whole other level of success."[4] Isn't it success if you show up authentically, rather than reluctantly? If you honor your need for rest, creativity, quiet, or to tend to our relationships with our children, our pets, our partners? Isn't it success when we accomplish a few tasks well, as opposed to several in mediocrity? Isn't it success to establish and honor our own boundaries? Indeed, it is.

Personally, I firmly believe it is a huge success and a sign of growth and progress when a woman does not feel the need to be liked. We spend so much time worrying about what other people think. We waste so much time making the exhausting effort to be pleasant. We smile so often at everything, to fight off the specter of Resting Bitch Face (RBF). We are expected to be nicer, lighter, more caring and compassionate than men. We are attributed with maternal tendencies as instinct, regardless of whether we have or have

> "One of the greatest regrets in life is being what others would want you to be, rather than being yourself."
>
> **SHANNON ALDER**

not had children. Instead of parading around the workplace smiling and waving like a pageant queen, don't you sometimes want to embrace the personality (and acceptance) of the grumpy old man? Grunts of frustration, the wave off from a backhand, impromptu naps, the unspecified bad mood – all permitted them, often in public, sometimes simultaneously!

Yet here we are, worried about our posture, our hair, the fit of our clothing, our smile, making eye contact, our shoes, sending holiday cards…or lack thereof and failure to do so. Where does it stop? So, you see, yes, the work of undoing is important. The work of undoing is the work of letting go of at least some of the gendered socialization and the expectations of others. The work of undoing is the work of becoming self-actualized, finally.

Before embracing assertiveness, you may need to spend some time grappling with clarity. I am fortunate enough to be friends (in real life!) with a remarkable clarity coach, Diana Morris (@dianaramorris), and I highly recommend her coaching sessions, workshops, and her most recent publication, *The Clarity Workbook*. Diana tells us why clarity matters:

> Clarity "allows us to take care of ourselves when we're faced with inevitable struggles and obstacles. It gives us metrics with which to make decisions and determine our next moves. It allows us to see through the fog. Clarity makes everything easier to understand."[5]

Certainly, you can work on both clarity and assertiveness at the same time. I could be persuaded that learning and exercising either one before the other might make sense. As I write today, I'm inclined to suggest pursuing clarity first and assertiveness thereafter, but to each their own. Both clarity coaching and assertiveness training are designed to help you build the life you want using the talents and gifts you have. I find it helpful to have clarity about my need to be assertive and my motivation to use assertiveness to accomplish my goals. Clarity can help you pinpoint where you are and help you identify what you need to do to move forward; assertiveness can help you get there. Again, Diana shares her wisdom: "Without a clear definition of your values and desires, you will spend precious time and energy working towards someone else's goals with very little to show for it." Assertiveness will help you lead your own life, as opposed to being swept along as a follower in the path of someone else.

Why are you where you are? Consider your life path thus far. Consider your career path. Consider your relationship history. Consider your health and wellbeing routines (or lack thereof). Would you confidently say that you feel that your life is of your own making? Or is life something that happens to you? These are fundamental questions, for the purposes of both clarity and assertiveness. You'll need to spend some time in reflection in order to truly identify, and perhaps, admit, to how much undoing there is to do in moving yourself toward the life that you want.

Consider this another way. Do you currently have the relationship that you think you deserve? Are you employed in a job that matches your interests, passions, and qualifications? Do you believe you are fairly paid in that job? Are you taking care of your physical and mental health? Why or why not? Do you feel confident that you will achieve your goals in the next 5-10 years? If not, why not?

Yes, again, we must confront our own present reality. What about your current conditions can you control? What is your responsibility for where you are right now? What prior decisions do you continue to feel bound by, that may be holding you back? Even if you are not ready to embrace the version of you that made those culminating decisions or failed to act, can you at least accept the facts about how you got where you are today? Can we accept the amazing version of you that already exists with strengths that can be maximized to drive you toward the future you are seeking?

I hope you find peace, acceptance, and compassion for all your prior selves. The good news is that people who do these periodic honest self-assessments and remain committed to personal growth often develop a more encompassing sense of self – one that can acknowledge one's imperfections. (Therapy helps, too!) You may even cultivate some self-compassion.

Consider the following page today's assignment. Try not to skip over this task. Spend a few minutes writing out your answers to the prompts outlined in Undoing Goals. I've even left the back of that page blank, in case you feel a strong urge to tear out the page and shred or burn it (safely), either to do so symbolically, in an act of closure, or to ensure your privacy.

THE WORK OF UNDOING

Undoing Goals

DATE:

In the boxes below, identify a primary goal in each category listed at left. Identify the most significant hurdle that remains in your way. Then, identify one action step you can take this week to begin the work of undoing.

CAREER/ EDUCATION	
ROMANTIC/ SEXUAL RELATIONSHIP	
FAMILY RELATIONS	
HEALTH & WELLBEING	
FINANCIAL	
OTHER _____	
OTHER _____	

Now, we need to talk about how you talk, about yourself, to and about others. A useful but, perhaps, painful exercise would be to watch yourself on video. Maybe some of you have had that pleasure before – this is a common practice among those working on improving their public speaking – but likely few of us have readily available footage of us engaging in our routine conversations, even if surveillance seems to be an aspect of our new normal. If you are using this book as a guide in a book club or with an accountability partner, you may want to take up this challenge and use your phone, tablet, or computer to record your next meeting or happy hour. You should only engage in such recording with the full knowledge and consent of all involved, however, and this agreement must also determine, in advance, how and when the recording will be utilized and destroyed. Misuse of such a recording would constitue aggressive or passive-aggressive harmful, untrustworthy behavior – certainly defying the aims and guidelines outlined here.

When listening to a recording of yourself proves too burdensome to obtain or to endure, other exercises will be necessary. In this case, internet searches and hashtags are your friend. While using your favorite app or search engine, useful terms to search might be *passive voice, assertive communication, passive aggressive communication, aggressive vs. assertive,* and so on. I recommend being specific, as searching #passive-aggressive may bring up posts of anger and sarcasm, and while some of those results may include hilarious memes, that may not be the best use of your time.

On the next page, you are provided with sample comments to evaluate for fairness and effectiveness. While you work through the examples, remember to be honest with yourself. Is the comment something you might say? If you believe you would respond differently, how? If you were trying to engage assertively, what might that sound like? Like any good teacher's daughter, I believe in homework. Spend a few minutes completing the exercise, Using Assertive Voice. We will next explore how to put your newfound assertive communication skills to work in your daily life.

Using Assertive Voice

Communicating assertively means speaking directly and owning our ideas and opinions. Assertive statements will almost always be stronger if written or spoken in active voice, rather than in passive voice. Note the actor and the actions in the sentences below. If the statement below feels passive, how could you rephrase?

It's fine. I don't want to inconvenience anyone.

☐ Assertive Voice
☐ Passive Voice

_____
_____
_____

I'm sorry, but would you mind taking out the recycling? I hate to be a bother, but they only pick up once a month.

☐ Assertive Voice   ☐ Passive Voice

_____
_____

I guess it doesn't matter if we're late; no one pays attention to me, anyway.

☐ Assertive Voice
☐ Passive Voice

_____
_____
_____

My car is always out of gas. (Said with a sigh to friends who sometimes borrow your car and don't refuel.)

☐ Assertive Voice
☐ Passive Voice

_____
_____

I am not comfortable when you say things like that.

☐ Assertive Voice
☐ Passive Voice

_____
_____
_____

NOTES:
_____
_____

CHAPTER FOUR

The Work of Doing: Get in There!

"In delay there lies no plenty."

— WILLIAM SHAKESPEARE —

Do you sometimes procrastinate? Or is procrastination a usual practice for you? If so, consider how that tendency is linked to assertiveness, or, rather, the lack thereof. Something is stopping you from going after your goal, from tackling the project, from even getting started. To start the work of doing, you must look inside to diagnose what the delay is all about. Living assertively means you sit down and do the thing. Enough already. Let's get started.

Timidity, hesitation, procrastination…these feelings are obstacles to assertive living. By now, you should have begun to identify some of the behaviors that have been holding you back. It is important to start now to build new practices to support your commitment to stepping up, standing out, and advocating for yourself and others. This requires self-discipline. Ugh. I know. The term makes me think of the most miserable forms of exercise, of conditioning. Yet building assertiveness skills is a journey no different than building any other type of proficiency. You have to practice, and you must practice regularly.

I remember being surprisingly moved and deeply inspired by the graduation speech delivered by Naval Admiral William H. McRaven, ninth commander of U.S. Special Operations Command, at the University of Texas--Austin Commencement on May 17, 2014. Since expanded into a book, this speech (which went viral) reinforces the necessity and wisdom of starting small and practicing often.

> It was a simple task – mundane at best. But every morning we were required to make our bed to perfection. It seemed a little ridiculous at the time, particularly in light of the fact that we were aspiring to be real warriors, tough battle-hardened SEALs, but the wisdom of this simple act has been proven to me many times over.

> If you make your bed every morning you will have accomplished the first task of the day. It will give you a small sense of pride, and it will encourage you to do another task and another and another. By the end of the day, that one task completed will have turned into many tasks completed. Making your bed will also reinforce the fact that little things in life matter. If you can't do the little things right, you will never do the big things right. And, if by chance you have a miserable day, you will come home to a bed that is made – that you made – and a made bed gives you encouragement that tomorrow will be better. If you want to change the world, start off by making your bed.[6]

THE WORK OF DOING: GET IN THERE!

You might be a person who makes your bed daily and now feels better about that practice. Or, you might be a person who irregularly makes your bed and made lighthearted fun of those who do so religiously. Obviously, the concept is broader than that literal practice, although I can confirm for you that I make my bed every single day. In business-speak, my brand is in alignment. My efforts to appear and actually be put together and influential start at home. Your work here does, as well.

It is unrealistic to expect to summon from great depths some unusual bravery to act (or react) assertively, instead of having cultivated skills readily available and at the surface. This means assertiveness skills can't be something kept in the back of the closet or buried in your handbag. Assertiveness is built and maintained by engaging in many minor routine practices that are necessary for taking care of yourself, so that you feel better physically, emotionally, and spiritually, if that's important to you. These practices of self-care will also guard against aggressiveness coming out in times when assertiveness would have served you better.

You make your bed. You take a shower. You brush your hair and brush your teeth. Take steps to neaten your appearance to whatever extent makes you feel like the best version of yourself. I dress strategically, based upon either what I need to accomplish each day or based upon how I want to feel that day. Somedays I want to be comfortable, and that's fine, too. But typically, I want to be persuasive, memorable, and appear competent and trustworthy. I dress for my most important meeting of the day. If the day poses a challenge, I dress in more streamlined, structured clothing, typically in solid "power" colors. This is an intentional practice. Sometimes, I dress assertively. When I need to be fierce, I wear red or black. When I want to seem kind and approachable, I wear softer colors or even something patterned or floral. I adjust my makeup similarly, varying color choices, coverage, and even placement on my face depending upon how pleasant or not I want to look that day.

So now I've made my bed and gotten ready and feel productive and prepared for what the day brings. And truth be told, coffee helps. If you do not have your morning routine down, now is the time. If instead you wake up late, throw your hair up in a messy bun, and throw on just anything that reasonably goes together and isn't too wrinkled for public wear, you may get yourself through the day, but you likely haven't positioned yourself for maximum impact in your community. How does your morning routine, your prep time, prepare you for your day? To summon assertiveness, remember, you must keep it accessible. When I'm tired, running late, need to put gas in the car, have to rush to a meeting, only to arrive frazzled and frumpy, I know I am not starting off fully present or invested in the task at hand. That meeting will only amount to the passage of time, as I wait for the minute to catch my breath that must wait until later. I do not perform well when that's how I start my day, and I am unlikely to set or accomplish my goals during life phases in which running late or on empty is the norm.

Living assertively means I also make time for lunch. Seriously – these easy, free actions are building blocks. Now, I do not mean a leisurely lunch and not even, necessarily, a healthy lunch, but at minimum, a lunch that gets the job done, so that I can avoid an afternoon slump or hunger-induced irritation or anger. I also know that I am happier and fresher for the work of the afternoon or evening, if I am able to get outside and take a bit of a break mid-day. For me, that translates into walking some place nearby, even if just a few steps outside of my office, and I try to do that when possible. Some of my colleagues prefer to bring their lunch from home and, they, too, benefit from a brief change of scenery mid-day, so we make time when we can to sit together at a table outside. To consistently make this happen, I strictly guard my own calendar and try to structure my days. Your situation may vary, and you can only control what you can control, but do what you can to deliberately construct your day to maximize your own productivity and wellbeing, with an eye toward thriving over the long haul.

Flexibility will be required. Routine is my preference, but adaptability is my friend. Some days, I eat a lousy microwave lunch alone at my desk, but only when that's the best option for successfully navigating the rest of my day. Making the decisions you need to make to get yourself through the day is assertive living, when you are making the best decisions that you can make for yourself, all things considered. Let's check in. Consider the following statements in the adjacent box. How many of these ring true for you?

 CHECK ALL THAT APPLY

- I GET OUT OF BED WHEN I NEED TO IN THE MORNING
- I DRESS INTENTIONALLY MOST OF THE TIME
- I ENGAGE IN REGULAR GROOMING AS NECESSARY FOR MY HEALTH AND WELL-BEING
- I LEAVE SOCIAL SITUATIONS WHEN I WANT TO AND AM NOT REGULARLY GUILTED INTO DOING THINGS I DON'T WANT TO DO BY MY FRIENDS
- I ASK MY SUPERVISOR FOR ASSIGNMENTS THAT INTEREST ME
- I FEEL ABLE TO SET BOUNDARIES WITH MY PARTNER OR ROOMMATE ABOUT SHARED SPACES IN OUR LIVING ENVIRONMENT
- IF I SHARE A KITCHEN OR BATHROOM WITH OTHERS AT WORK, I CONTRIBUTE REGULARLY KEEPING IT CLEAN
- I REGULARLY GET MYSELF TO WORK ON TIME
- I EAT FOOD THAT I ENJOY AND/OR IS GOOD FOR ME MOST OF THE TIME
- I PARTICIPATE IN DECISION-MAKING IN MY FRIEND GROUP WHEN WE MAKE PLANS
- I FEEL COMFORTABLE ASKING FOR TIME OFF WORK
- I TELL MY SUPERVISOR WHEN I NEED MORE TIME OR SUPPORT FOR AN ASSIGNMENT
- IF I SHARE A BED WITH SOMEONE, I GET HALF OF ITS SPACE AND SHEETS AND BLANKETS
- IF I SHARE A FRIDGE WITH COLLEAGUES, I GET MY FAIR SHARE OF SPACE AND MY FOOD IS NOT REGULARLY EATEN BY OTHERS

How many of the items on this checklist prompted an easy yes for you? Work through the items and identify what obstacles lie in your way for any answers that came up short of an unqualified yes. Actively and honestly consider what may be holding you back.

Living assertively means you take stock and take ownership of your life. This means that we must also embrace its responsibilities. Balance is key to evaluating whether or not you have ventured into aggressiveness or selfishness. You should not feel entitled to space in the refrigerator at work, for example, if you do not also wipe it out and regularly throw out your old food and take home your dirty dishes. Remember, there is a difference between aggressive and assertive living – and the world needs no more selfish, entitled, greedy people.

With that balance in mind, how do the following statements make you feel?

- I feel a sense of ownership in my home
- I feel a sense of belonging in my workplace
- I believe I am in an egalitarian romantic relationship
- I believe I get out what I put into my friendships
- I feel sufficiently understood and accepted by my family
- I believe I am demonstrating my worth at work
- I believe my appearance reflects how I feel about myself

Consider your reaction to reading each statement above. For each, answer the following questions: Why, or why not? Then identify three steps you could take that would strengthen your position within each of those relationships. Were your thoughts and answers reactive or proactive? Did you think first of what you could do, or did you think of how the other person needed to change? Remember to focus on what *you* can control. There is certainly a time and place for negotiating and advocating for yourself within relationships, but assertive living means approaching a situation with a sense of agency and capability. Is life what happens to you, or do you think of life as what you make it?

As it turns out, our bodies can tell us a lot about when we are or are not living assertively.

In her book, *Running on Empty: Overcome your Childhood Emotional Neglect*, Jonice Webb, PhD, outlines connections between non-assertiveness in adulthood and experiences of childhood emotional neglect.[7] Webb explains how adults who may have experienced great physical care may have still experienced emotional neglect in childhood, resulting in an inability to engage in healthy emotional processing and regulation in adulthood. This inability or inadequacy may show up in the body in a variety of ways, from tension headaches to bodily aches and pains, to restless legs, hand-wringing, hair loss, and more. The work of undoing, of unlearning some concepts and cultivating new skills, may very well improve your health and wellbeing, both physical and mental. Another book worth reading is *The Body Keeps the Score: Brain, Mind, and Body in the Healing of Trauma* by Bessel van der Kolk, M.D.[8] Learning to engage with others assertively may help you feel peaceful and satisfied at the end of the day, allowing the shoulders to drop, jaw to unclench, and mind to rest, as you know that you did your best today to advocate for yourself and others. As we learn to let out those inner thoughts, our body can begin to release and unwind, as assertive engagement means that we stop holding it all inside of us.

Before reading further, take some time to work through the exercises that close this chapter. These exercises are designed to help you convince yourself that assertiveness building is work worth doing. Once you have completed the exercises, you can revisit your answers when your confidence is wavering and as new obstacles arise. Tough tasks are often worth undertaking, and we will next explore how to guard against the temptation of taking the easy way out.

DROWNING IN TIMIDITY

DATE:

Assertiveness Pros and Cons

Often, we let our minds get carried away with possible worst-case scenario outcomes when something less monumental is much likelier to occur. Consider something that you are worried about, in anticipation, or that recently annoyed you. What would the benefits of confronting the situation assertively be? What are likely -- not possible, but likely--negative repercussions for not responding assertively?

Pros

Cons

Reflection

Evaluation

THE WORK OF DOING: GET IN THERE!

THE BODY SPEAKS

For one week, make note of minor irritations, arguments, bad news, new tasks, or moments of uncertainty that may arise. How did your tendency toward non-assertiveness show up in your body? Note where in the body you noticed a physical reaction to the stressor, when it appeared, and what impact the physiological response had on the rest of your day.

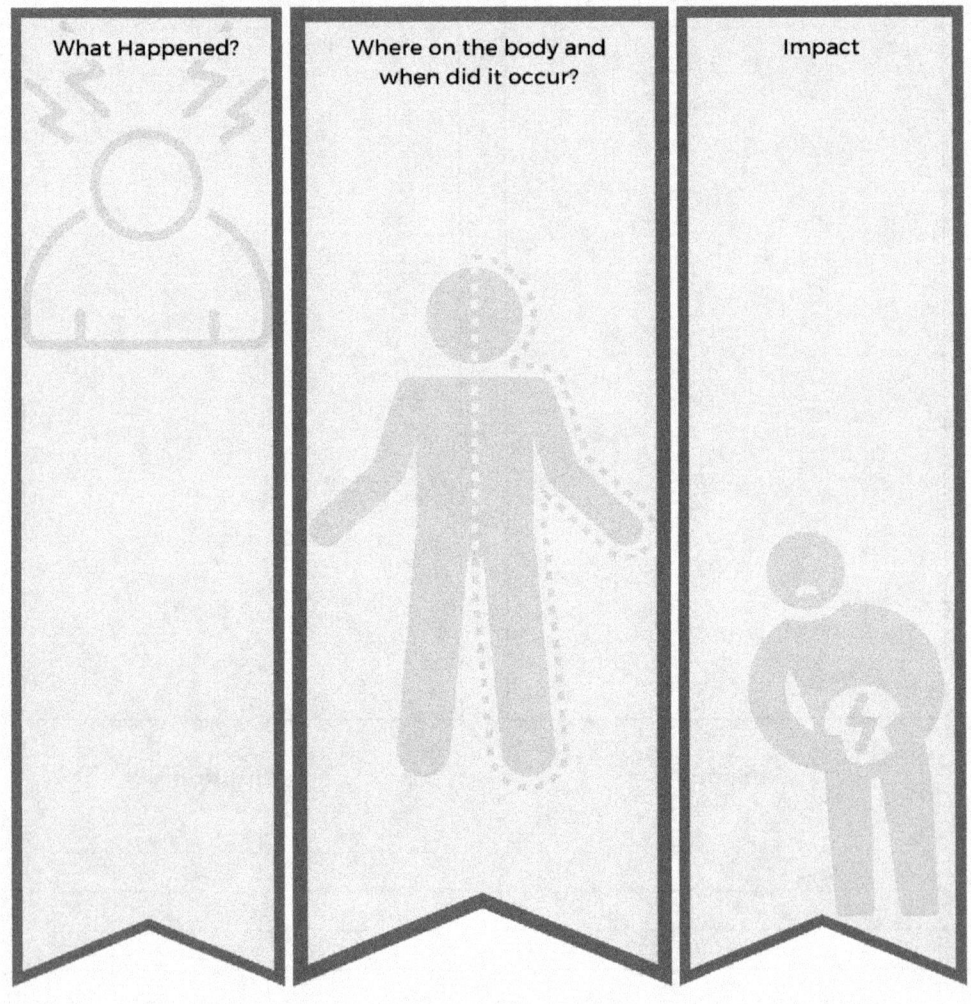

| What Happened? | Where on the body and when did it occur? | Impact |

CHAPTER FIVE

Guarding Against Taking the Easy Way Out (or Assertiveness as Allyship)

> *"You show people what you're willing to fight for when you fight your friends."*
>
> — Hillary Clinton —

Sometimes on an assertiveness-building journey, we find ourselves tempted to slip back into avoidance and conciliatory behaviors, following the accomplishment of our initial goal. Maybe you just successfully negotiated for a raise or asked for a more permanent flex or remote work schedule, now that the recent pandemic has convinced many employers to reconsider their former workplace norms and practices. Good for you! Like the rest of us, you may have been raised and socialized to smooth out wrinkles, both in clothing and conversation. Now, when a generation-plus of women have embraced the opportunity to engage more fully in nearly all aspects of society, we are learning and unlearning, growing bolder, and may find ourselves in opportunities to use our assertiveness skills for greater purpose. Admittedly, sometimes using our "soft skills," such as playing the mediator may be useful, and when mediation is strategic and employed to help accomplish some other goal besides making ourselves feel more comfortable (which is different from unsafe – more on that later), there is nothing wrong with the method per se; however, you and I know that women *frequently* make nice, even insincerely, just to reduce or move past conflict.

Conflict is healthy. And, it is inevitable. So, our decision becomes this – are we going to engage and assert our own rights and wants and wellbeing? Are we going to engage and assert ourselves on behalf of the rights and wants and needs of others? Or, are we going to let others continue to put themselves first and champion their own causes or agenda at our and others' expense? To practice and work toward assertive living, we must acknowledge the existence of conflict, learn to coexist with conflict, and begin to work with it to improve women's lives and the lives of others.

White women, in particular, are prone to retreating into the shield of politeness rather than confronting discomfort, bullying, discrimination, injustice, or any number of situations and behaviors that warrant intervention. How often is this politeness an excuse for inaction? For our complicity? As our television and computer screens are filled with images of people in pain and asking for change, where are you? Reading uncomfortably right now? Upset that I've gone there so soon in this chapter, or glad to see it? Either way – this chapter is for you. To live assertively and authentically, I believe that I must also be increasingly committed to anti-racist, anti-discrimination efforts, education, and action, and I hope you do, too. The year 2020 fully convinced me that it is white women who are most prone to drowning in timidity, and the consequences for all of us are *dire*.

I've been guilty of the same inaction before. I have witnessed and allowed plenty of offensive, harmful, or risky behaviors to occur in my midst and failed to address them how or when I should have. Again, please sit for a moment in discomfort, if it has found you. The goal here is to acknowledge and confront our collective reality and shift our thinking and behavior for both our self-improvement and also for the collective good. The proof of both lingering effects of past discrimination and contemporary effects of ongoing racism is everywhere, and the majority of White people have tolerated and avoided addressing this for far too long, author included. What I am asking you, reader, to do here is continue on in your path that led you to pick up this book. See the tough conversations through. Be strong enough to become the sincerely good person that you want to be. Remember, the Good Samaritan did something. The helping is what makes them the Good Samaritan. Know that merely believing in equality and justice is not enough. We must engage in the work of bringing it about, building it into our homes and offices and organizations. People write policies and make the rules and enforce them – or don't. People choose to allow the continuation of violence and inequity – or don't. People look the other way for decades when discriminatory harms such as sexual assault, for example, occur time and time again, within our churches and schools. People choose to uphold institutional reputations over their proclaimed institutional values, existing in hypocrisy and conflict, while wringing their hands and telling themselves or others that there is nothing they can do. I cannot let you off the hook here. These protestations and common excuses are simply not true. There is always something we can do. Always. Something.

Always.

Both the inexperienced and disempowered can get lost in their own feelings of inadequacy yet feel drawn into big-picture thinking, hoping to solve the broader problem by identifying some quick, magic solution, instead of envisioning the power (with its potential far-reaching effects) that their own smaller, individual actions may have. As with many problem-solving techniques, the key to moving past this assertiveness block is to break the larger concern into smaller pieces. What can you do where you are with what you've got?

Friendly reminder – the wonderful deep well of the internet is your friend. During a recent workshop I co-facilitated on conducting difficult conversations, participants shared the usefulness of several existing techniques pulled from a range of disciplines and professions, all of them interesting and relevant to our purposes here. In many ways, assertive living is simply a series of difficult conversations. Even when a situation may call for action first, a discussion almost certainly follows. But most of the time, the assertive act or decision will begin simply with the choice and commitment to speak your concern, needs, or boundaries into existence. So, I recommend that you engage in some creative internet searching for communication tools of particular relevance to you. Although I am not typically trying to sell a product, I have found empathy mapping[9] incredibly helpful. A tool of design-thinking often used to help imagine the potential or ideal customer, empathy mapping is broadly applicable to any interaction with another person or group.

Another set of tools may be drawn from healthcare providers, many of whom must regularly deliver, at best, tough love, or, at worst, terminal diagnoses to patients. Nurses have refined a variety of techniques to help them coach people into engaging in healthier behaviors while also managing the emotions of the patient and the patient's family. Now that's a tough job and years of practice we can learn from! The SPIKES model often used in healthcare settings is one example.[10] SPIKES is an acronym, and, to summarize, the model suggests the following steps: **S**et up the conversation, try to gauge the patient's existing knowledge of or **P**erception of condition and its seriousness, solicit an **I**nvitation from the patient to hear more about the condition, provide **K**nowledge to the patient (medical facts), explore the patient's **E**motions and sympathize with the patient and family, and close the conversation with a summary and **S**trategy for care.

Another method of using and modeling assertiveness at work is through active bystander intervention. By definition, the active bystander (as compared with the passive bystander) is assertive. The active bystander acts. The active bystander is the person who chooses to do something, rather than nothing, and that choice can make all the difference to our fellow humans and to a larger family, community, or workplace culture.

Bystander intervention has become common on college and university campuses, particularly since 2014, as a result of increased awareness and scrutiny of the frequent nature of sexual assault occurring on or around college campuses. Certainly, if we expect teens and young adults to display such courage, we should expect the same of ourselves. As with any new exercise, practice makes perfect. It's okay to start by learning, but to build confidence in intervening, it is important to run through scenarios, brainstorm possible actions you could take, and practice those interactions, particularly if you were raised to mind your own business, avoid interrupting people, and avoid conflict. Bystander intervention requires intervention, after all, and while it has been piloted to address epidemic levels of sexual assault, both its research foundation and its practice may be applied to a variety of risky situations and problematic behaviors. Notably, these trainings have already begun to be expanded to address incivility, sexual harassment, and racism in employment and educational environments. We should take these lessons and apply them to our lives broadly.

Bystander intervention asks us to engage in the world around us by doing more – more noticing, more caring, more confronting, and more problem-solving. The idea is that we, as humans simply navigating life on this planet, are always potential helpers for one another. As so many gaps in services exist, often disproportionately, across our communities, it is often unrealistic to rely upon a designated expert intervener-rescuer for the many types of concerning situations we may witness. How many times have you been the passive bystander who did not know what to do? How many times have you witnessed an escalating argument, an imbalance of power, or a racist joke, and done nothing? The assertive person confronts their own inaction and inability to respond with an eye towards handling the situation differently and more proactively in the future. Bystander intervention training can teach you these skills.

To start, you need to identify what the warning signs are of the harm or behavior you are hoping to prevent. In a focused training, your facilitator will work through these warning signs with participants. If you are working on your own, again, the internet can be your guide. For example, an internet search for "warning signs of domestic violence" usually yields a credible list of national advocacy organizations that offer help for those experiencing domestic violence but also information for those wishing to learn how to help. Some of the tips offered are forms of bystander intervention, although these outreach efforts are not always labeled as such. Asking a friend about a bruise on their arm can be an act of bystander intervention and doing so requires us to have the nerve to ask – hence the assertiveness-bystander intervention connection.

Consider your many everyday interactions that are quite ripe for intervention that routinely go unaddressed. Perhaps you have heard the term *microaggressions*. Many of us and our friends and colleagues experience countless microaggressions outside of the home, whether at school or work or church, or even at the grocery store or while putting gas in our car. Now, if you are White, middle or upper class, identify as male, cisgender, and/or heterosexual, you are less likely to be the target of microaggressions, and, as a result, more likely to discount their prevalence and impact.[11] But if you hold a type of privilege, friends, hear me – you do not get to decide how to weigh the impact of discrimination on those who do not share in that particular type of privilege. That should be obvious, but clearly (see the U.S. in 2020), it is not. In White majority countries, the prevalence and harms of racism are discounted. In male-dominated workplaces, sexism is discounted. In societies built around heterosexuality, same-sex relationships and practices are discounted. In a nation built upon the idea of equal rights, well, hypocrisy is all around us. Discrimination permeates the everyday. Micro and macro aggressions are common, and they are apt opportunities for assertive bystander intervention.

Typically, these intervention trainings offer a handful of engagement strategies. I want to introduce the top five intervention tactics I have found most useful and most likely to be used. You may confront a situation directly, create a distraction, recruit others to help you, delegate responding to someone more empowered to help, create a delay in the risk of harm, and you can document what it is occurring. As bystander intervention programs continue to grow, more solutions will be developed, so you should revisit training from time to time. It is important to note that there is no hierarchy of the tactics. What is most important is to do something more than passively observing. Keep in mind that there is no neutral position. Silence and inaction are forms of toleration. Silence and inaction are certainly not assertive behaviors. Where inaction is likely from our training and socialization, we must purposefully engage in active unlearning. Changing our mind is not enough; we must also change our behavior.

COMMUNITY RESPONSIBILITY

5 Intervention Tactics

- Confront a situation directly
- Create some sort of distraction that disrupts the moment
- Delegate the responsibility for responding to someone with more authority, expertise, or capability to address the situation (not necessarily police)
- Using one of the other tactics, try to create a delay, to help dissipate tensions, separate those involved in the conflict, and/or allow others to respond
- Document what you witnessed and offer to verify the victim or target's experience

Allyship is Assertiveness in Action.

Another important consideration when evaluating your intervention options is your own personal safety. Sometimes, the risk is worth taking. But bystander intervention does not ask us to pretend we are invincible. And if heroism is what you are imagining, you're aiming too high. In the trainings, many participants assume they are supposed to say that they will confront a situation directly. That would be the brave choice, they think, and bravery is an American ideal. However, direct confrontation is also the least likely to occur, particularly among those new to bystander training. The more you were raised to mind your own business, the less likely you are to intervene directly, especially if you do not know the people involved very well. Self-awareness becomes important here – you must begin to truly know yourself to recognize what you will and will not likely do. Diagnosing your own tendencies and personal obstacles ahead of time will help you more quickly filter through the available options when you find yourself confronted with a situation to address.

When intervening, we know that context matters. You may feel entirely comfortable confronting your sibling or friend directly about their behavior but might find doing so with your boss or mother-in-law impossible. You may identify as an introvert and as someone deeply afraid of public conflict, so perhaps delegating is the best option for you. In a party environment, we have found that college students feel better able to respond when they can recruit friends to intervene alongside them, and they prefer to use the distraction method if and when they can. Here, they may choose to lean into existing gender norms, with women asking women friends to go to the bathroom with them, which is considered socially acceptable, or men may tell another man that his car is getting towed. Such distractions may create the opportunity to separate two intoxicated friends they are worried about or be used to separate a friend, intoxicated or not, from someone they think may pressure or try to take advantage of them later. Those of us well past high school and college should take lessons from these attempts of young adults. In tackling a wide swath of issues of social justice, Millennials and Generation Z are impressively leading.

Remember that delegating and documenting are fine options. Delegating responsibility to act to someone more likely to be successful and documenting what happened are both ways for you to do something, rather than nothing. Again, context matters. Consider when it is appropriate to call police and consider when that would be an overreaction. Consider if the race or ethnicity of those involved is factoring into that impulse for you, and if it should. If you are witnessing a crime, consider that using your phone to audio or video record the situation could be helpful to the target or victim afterwards. However, you should never share or post a recording of violence or discrimination on social media without the permission of the person harmed. That would not be an act of bystander intervention – that could be an invasion of privacy that could cause more harm than good. Do what you can, where you are, with what you've got, and do it sincerely and responsibly.

Most of the time, the situations suitable for your intervention will not pose such high stakes. Instead, all we truly need to do is learn to survive a little discomfort. You can. You do, in fact, with all too much regularity. What if we could learn to introduce that discomfort, wield it and endure it, strategically and for the greater good? Strong leaders, the people you think of as successful, have mastered this, and you can, too. Picture those mentors, world leaders, and television characters that are assertiveness role models for you. Chances are those people who came to mind not only act boldly – they also take the heat that sometimes follows those bold acts. Whether I am talking to people about negotiating salary or setting boundaries with their family about holiday plans, the same directive applies – after you assert your wants and needs, you also must hold firm. Sometimes, holding firm means sitting in silence for a few moments; sometimes, the silent treatment may last a few days or weeks. Remember, you cannot control the reaction of the other party. Remember that their reaction is not your responsibility. Remind yourself that their reaction does not mean that your wants and needs are not valid. Your ask is certainly worthy of consideration, especially if you are trying to negotiate with someone close to you. Remind yourself that they should care about how you feel and what you think is best and just for you in that relationship. They should care. Sadly, that doesn't mean they will, or that they will come to that realization on your preferred timeline. If you are just now beginning to assert yourself in a relationship that had already settled into a usual routine, with routine behaviors on all sides, the readjustment period may be rough. Restructuring your relationship may take some time. Embracing passivity could feel like the easy way out and appear increasingly appealing, particularly if you are interacting with someone you believe has the "stronger personality" or "cares more." Truth be told, they probably do not actually care more, although they may care the loudest. Stop rewarding their bad behavior. In the space carved out through these negotiations and your moments of holding firm, you may come to realize how selfish or manipulative people sometimes are. You may begin to see much more clearly how others have relied upon your conciliatory nature and your need to please others. Enough, women, with all the performed pleasantness! This gendered default position of politeness may rear its fake smiling (but not necessarily ugly) head time and time again. Assertiveness is a practice, and sometimes you will need to periodically revisit the fundamentals. Stop pasting a fake smile on your face, keep your guard up against your impulse to take the easy way out, and practice sitting in discomfort in increasing increments of time. You'll soon find that you can survive the unpleasant phone call, the tense meeting, the rough patch with a friend. And you will also come out the other side being treated more fairly. You will come out feeling better about those moments of conflict, especially when you push through them on behalf of others. Assertiveness, as with many facets of women's empowerment, can offer a win-win scenario, individually and collectively, if we keep up the practice. Enduring the tensions of personal growth and acts of bystander intervention will certainly pay off for all of us in the long run.

GUARDING AGAINST TAKING THE EASY WAY OUT

You know that asking for time off work is worth the joy of vacation. Similarly, forcing yourself to negotiate your salary is worth the raise. Addressing conflict is worth the peace of resolution. Take it from those of us who have made it to the other side. The strength built over time spent in assertiveness practice feels good. Assertiveness feels good! Whether you find it easier to work on yourself or to deploy assertiveness on behalf of others, there is no wrong way to start. The call to action is this – don't keep the benefits of assertiveness to yourself. Pay it forward. Engage authentically and sincerely in the social issues you say you care about. Injustice is all around us, and the issues are urgent. Assertiveness is required for us to be that change the world so desperately needs.

DROWNING IN TIMIDITY

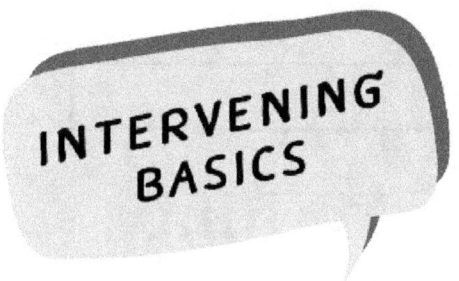

DATE:
_____

In the space below, write out your concerns, obstacles, and motivation for practicing and engaging in acts of bystander intervention.

- When thinking about myself as a potential active, intervening bystander, I am most concerned about:

  _____
  _____
  _____

- However, I know it is important to intervene because:

  _____
  _____
  _____

- I believe that I can overcome my fears and insecurities about intervening by:

  _____
  _____
  _____

- When researching communication styles, I found the following types or tools that I may use:

  _____
  _____
  _____

GUARDING AGAINST TAKING THE EASY WAY OUT

DATE

Assertive Writing

Take a position on a hot-button political issue and support it as strongly as you can.

Sample topics: sexual harassment, reproductive rights, racial inequality, your salary, parental leave, healthcare, immigration, the Presidential election, etc.

DROWNING IN TIMIDITY

Reread your response. Draw a line through any apologetic or tentative language. Circle any words that convey emphasis, conviction, or passion. Reread your writing. Are you persuaded?

CHAPTER SIX

Embracing Fear, Insecurity, and Uncertainty

*"Success is not final, failure is not fatal:
it is the courage to continue that counts."*

— Winston Churchill —

Those of us who engage with the world assertively also experience fear. We hesitate, doubt ourselves, struggle to trust others, and wonder if our efforts our worth the hassle. Yet we do it anyway. In recent years, I was fortunate enough to be nominated for my workplace's leadership program for promising future company leaders. The nomination was recognition and considered an honor, and I was simultaneously flattered and nervous. Typically, these types of programs, particularly in the U.S., are heavily geared toward extroverts. And if you aren't one already, well, then the point is to make you one by the time you come out! Joking aside, I survived, and it was not as bad as I thought (life will teach you that these kinds of experiences rarely are), and, indeed, the months-long program spawned growth, opportunity, and fostered wonderful new and strong friendships with caring, compassionate, kick-ass women (and some good men, too). The greatest insight from this program (which to date I also consider the greatest compliment I have ever received) came through the use of 360-degree assessments, completed by our supervisors and colleagues. These were conducted early in the leadership program, and I believe my results struck the program's leaders by surprise. Truth be told, the results surprised me, as well, but this exercise helped me view and know myself more concretely – a much-needed gift at that point in my career. Pam, one of this program's exceptional leaders, met with each of us to discuss our results. Pam pulled my results from the yellow envelope and told me that I had scored highest on courage, and she smiled and shared that courage was rarely someone's top quality, even among the varied participants in this type of leadership program. This news delighted me to no end, but aside from telling my husband about this pleasant conversation during my workday, I initially was hesitant to share this flattering finding with others, for fear of sounding self-important and self-congratulatory. So here I was, a campus leader in a leadership program simultaneously prioritizing and perpetuating women's self-effacing nature. Only months later, after intense work in the leadership program and sustained conflict and stress in my role, did I come to understand – courage is why I am here. Courage is what I've got. Courage is what made me a leader, and courage is what warranted the recognition. At the same time, I was surrounded by people displaying a lack of courage; multiple people failing to work courageously, with disastrous consequences. By then, I had also witnessed firsthand many of the men in this program, most of them both older and higher-ranking in our workplace hierarchy, struggle with insecurity, self-consciousness, and self-doubt. Some men struggled through the days devoted to navigating conflict. Some of the women did, too, but I already knew why. (So do you, that's why we're here.) Some of the men did not prove themselves to be quite the leaders

EMBRACING FEAR, INSECURITY, AND UNCERTAINTY

we thought them to be, or that they thought of themselves. I don't share this here to be petty. Plenty of men are exceptional leaders. I share this to point out that, sadly, in a patriarchy, even self-identified feminists (that's me) still find themselves unconsciously believing the hype. We had assumed men's leadership capabilities first and doubted them later, when women experience the reverse. I share this anecdote here because this was the months-long journey that finally freed me from the last vestiges of imposter syndrome. While some portions of the leadership program were rough, I hung in there; when some portions were rough for others, I shined. I began seeing and believing in my courage and understanding how it has propelled my career. I can tell you firsthand that courage is different from confidence, although I believe it is likely that one eventually can produce the other. Confidence is believing you can do something; courage is believing you must, despite the risk.

Yes, I have courage in droves, but why had it taken me so long to learn that about myself? Why had I found all the other words to describe my behavior, including plenty of negative ones (e.g., bossy), instead? Why did I believe courage belonged, for example, to the former military men in our leadership program, only to discover they sometimes didn't have it in our workplace (far from the battlefield), in matters in which I did? It was a transformative work year, the combination of heavy role-specific challenges occurring while I was also participating in this program. The year was tough but rewarding. I now embrace the word *courage* and use it to describe myself. I use it intentionally, particularly when working with groups that continue to tightly grip traditional or stereotypical gender norms and strive to reinforce the gender binary. What does it mean for men to consider me as a face of courage? What does it mean to the women to know courage is a characteristic also available to them – that courage is a necessity?

Yes, I am courageous, yet I still experience nervousness, uncertainty, hesitation, and even the dreaded caring what people think. Yet I engage assertively anyway. During a now famous talk Michelle Obama gave in London on December 3, 2018, our former First Lady told the audience that yes, even still, she experienced bouts of imposter syndrome. When asked how it felt to be considered a symbol of hope, she said:

> I still have a little imposter syndrome, it never goes away, that you're actually listening to me. It doesn't go away, that feeling that you shouldn't take me that seriously. What do I know? I share that with you because we all have doubts in our abilities, about our power and what that power is.[12]

When then asked about what advice she might offer younger women, she continued:

> My advice to young women is that you have to start by getting those demons out of your head….I have been at probably every powerful table that you can think of, I have worked at nonprofits, I have been at foundations, I have worked in corporations, served on corporate boards, I have been at G-summits, I have sat in at the U.N.: They are not that smart.[13]

You might then discover that with courage comes power. You might then be able to tap into feelings of power you did not know were inside of you, and you may cultivate more power than you ever knew you could wield. Again, we must remember that we should be building this power through assertiveness – not aggressiveness. Similarly, we then should make good use of that power, and not engage in abuses of power. My preferred description of power comes from Martin Luther King, Jr., who shared, in his 1967 book, *Where Do We Go From Here: Chaos or Community:*

> Power, properly understood, is the ability to achieve purpose. It is the strength required to bring about social, political or economic changes. In this sense power is not only desirable but necessary in order to implement the demands of love and justice…What is needed is a realization that power without

love is reckless and abusive and that love without power is sentimental and anemic. Power at its best is love implementing the demands of justice. Justice at its best is love correcting everything that stands against love.[14]

Quite simply, power may be defined as the ability to achieve purpose. In that sense, power is not so scary. We all want to achieve purpose. Assertiveness can help you build the influence you will need to achieve purpose. Assertiveness becomes self-perpetuating in this way – you build influence, you gain power, you use your power to achieve purpose, and with proven results, you are likely to get the chance again. You receive recognition for your talents and skills, and your influence expands; you gain followers. I urge you to use your growing assertiveness and influence for good. When this all comes together – that, indeed, is the life worth living. You might even find yourself getting paid for doing what you love! Once you gain experience and establish yourself in your field or workplace, you will find yourself asserting yourself without thinking about it, without anticipatory anxiety, without waves of imposter syndrome, with confidence in your decisions and a sense of certainty about what and how you do what you do. That stage is sometimes described as flow, and what you have found is a calling. Trust me, that feeling Martin Luther King, Jr., articulated in the excerpt above – "Power at its best is love implementing the demands of justice," – that kind of work, that type of power ... that feeling is unmatched. If life gets in the way of your ability to make your calling your full-time job, then let your paid labor support your activism or volunteer work. What is the work that you are called to do? Where do you tend to be when that inner voice of courage strives to come out? Apply your assertiveness skills and exert yourself in that arena, and you may come to truly believe that work may, in fact, be its own reward. This type of work is very fulfilling, and assertiveness can help you find it. As Honoré de Balzac says, "All happiness depends on courage and work."[15]

There are those (and they are plenty; mostly white and mostly male), who will argue that the work of social justice is unnecessarily divisive, that identity politics (which they consider a negative term), and political correctness have ruined something (take your pick), and that those identities claiming to experience a form of discrimination or oppression are wallowing in victimhood. Whether one uses those terms or not, such arguments can be found around every corner – in the classroom, on the news, on Twitter, on Facebook, on Instagram. The contemporary version of (the white, heterosexual, cisgender) man's (genuinely desperate) search for meaning appears to be leading him to provocative authoritarian "thought leaders." In this line of thinking, every white man is an individual; everyone else belongs to their collective identity group, and they belong there due to weakness, passivity, or incompetence, so the argument goes. I find myself increasingly rebutting these ideas both in and outside of the classroom, including from among white liberal men who consider themselves allies to many movements. For those of us who have been around for decades now, we know these claims are not new, but I am concerned because the rapid embracing of these ideas by white men across the spectrum of economic status and stability is new (again) and growing. The proponents of this men's rights agenda welcome women, some of whom are finding this rhetoric attractive, and they will welcome Black men and Latino men and other men of color without pause, as long as those folks will overlook the explicitly racist and sexist themes that emerge in the leaders' speeches and writings, whether in best-selling non-fiction books or Reddit subthreads. And plenty do, clinging to the voices of firm direction that fill the void that is every young man's quest to meet the impossible standards of masculinity, especially in these challenging times in which their assumed gender-based birthright (in a patriarchy) is being resisted left and right. More so left, admittedly. As I've said, I find myself drawn into these conversations far more than I would like – it isn't pleasant, and simply mentioning it here may mean I will find myself subject to a phase of online harassment, if it comes to their attention – but I can't ignore this rhetoric because it makes a mockery of victimization, and I work every day with victims. Victims who are woefully misrepresented and misunderstood, conveniently so, by those who belong to the identity who engage in the most typical types of harm.

   I suppose these men would like everyone to believe that this is all coincidence – that men commit the overwhelming majority of sexual assaults, despite the gender identity of the person harmed. That women disproportionately experience sexual and dating and domestic violence. That Black and Brown women experience disproportionately high rates of violence. That it is coincidence that the most toxic, most environmentally contaminating processing plants just so happen to exist in the parts of town less populated by white middle and upper-class families. That the justice system just so happens to convict Black men at shockingly high rates, while acquitting white men for similar crimes for which there was similar evidence. That Native Americans just so happen to experience high suicide, domestic violence, and alcohol misuse rates for no reason at all, as if there is no connection to the genocide white men conducted upon "discovering" the land that has become the United States. As if white men and women haven't lied and cheated and reneged upon treaty after treaty, forced various non-white populations into concentration camps (by any name) and then pretended to be benevolent while ensuring that those people were not provided with sufficient food, clothing, blankets, toilets, showers, medicine and other medical care, and then pretend that their white supremacy (as long as you don't say it out loud!) is due to some actual innate or Christian God-given superiority instead of incredible moral failing, deceit, and self-deception (which surely disappoints that same god). This is not "liberal propaganda." These are facts. These things are taught in the same history books common in U.S. public education for those of us who grew up in the 60s, 70s, 80s, 90s, and 2000s. The question is whose point of view do you take? What lies do you tell yourself to fill in the gaps? What questions don't you ask?

You cannot pretend that you believe all people are created equal and then treat them so differently, unequally distribute resources, and then blame others for the result. So many white men and plenty of white women find libertarianism attractive for these reasons. White people get to pretend that this all began when all things were equal, and then they attribute white supremacy to white superiority, which they often call "competence." And sure, libertarianism sounds appealing, when you are sitting safe, and warm, fed and clothed, with a safety net of some sort (no yacht required), in a political science classroom, comparing and contrasting one political theory against another, considering what type of society you might choose, *all things being equal.* I engaged in those thought exercises when I was a young political science major during my undergraduate years. And sure, hypothetically, libertarianism can sound very appealing. But apparently, when you are white and male, it can be far too easy to assume that the conditions are equal and every human gets to start from the same starting line to establish themselves. This is the so-called "American Dream," after all. They never stop to ask, but we will. Whose dream is it? For whom is this actually attainable?

Working in higher education, I have participated in various step-forward/step-back walk of discrimination and oppression learning activities over the years. Who do you think ends up angry, consistently, during these things? Participants are asked questions about their life experiences – their own individual, true, factual, actually experienced life experiences – and simply step forward or back if they did or did not experience the situation described in the question. Who do you think ends up in the front, the middle, the back of the room? But who is so mad about being in the front?

Now, this writing should not be taken as an endorsement of these activities. Context matters, and it *crucially* matters who is conducting the exercise and what language is used in the questions, and how participants' emotions are managed (or not). Often, an individual white man will say, "But I've worked hard!" And yes, they likely have. They fail to see that their work ethic is not what the exercise is about. "But I've worked hard" = "But I deserve it!" even though they typically try to avoid saying it that way. But the next thing deliberately left unsaid is, "and you don't" and "you must not have worked as hard as I have," despite incredible evidence to the contrary.

The questions are not typically about what effort you have made to advance your own career. The questions are about life experiences and conditions that should rationally and often do exist as hurdles to one's advancement. Routinely, there are also often white men who marvel at finding themselves in the middle-back, who are astonished to learn something about their life that they had not realized before. The last time I participated in one of these exercises, the white man next to me, likely in his mid-forties, was visibly lost in thought. He later explained to a small group of participants that he just then realized that his family had received "government cheese," a form of financial support from the government that his mother had explained away during his childhood, in an effort to make both the getting and the using of the food subsidy as fun and as palatable as possible. His up-to-that-moment belief in American meritocracy had obscured his own understanding of his childhood socioeconomic status, his family's status in relation to others, and his own achievement as based to the limits (he heretofore believed) of his own capacity. What might be the benefits enjoyed by the family with an abundance of food (nutrition) and the time not spent in navigating the bureaucracy that we put families in need through? Surely, we can, in our most rational calculations understand that time and effort matter in terms of production. Sadly, this holds true whether we're talking about widgets or children.

Given prevailing gender norms, I doubt too many men are at this point in this book, if they picked it up at all, but if still with me, you may be bristling. You may be tempted to quit at this point and put the book down in frustration. I wouldn't be surprised. Many men I work with and many young men I have in the classroom come to me with the "Why do women…" questions. I think they enjoy the topic, enjoy some debate, for sport, but then stop enjoying the answer, when it inevitably emerges and links to patriarchy in some way. This seems to hold true, whether I use the word "patriarchy" or not, although certainly, using the word quickens and strengthens the resistance from time to time. Earlier today, before working on this chapter, I had a high intensity conversation with a former male student (very well educated, very intelligent, well-read, good natured) about the stark gender divide in the initiation of divorce. The conversation began with a sincere question, but it ended in uncomfortable disagreement. Why do more women initiate divorce? He suggested that women "get bored" and are "far more capricious." No research on his part, no data, just some white male instinct about the inherent nature of women that he wanted to believe, despite being confronted with overwhelming credible evidence to the contrary. Any study or source I offered that addressed the question was rejected. Why believe sound sociological and psychological research, longitudinal marital satisfaction studies, or your trusted gender studies professor, when you could simply land on blaming women? Instead, let's go with Eve got bored. I remain concerned because here he is, one of the future leaders of America – convinced that women can't be trusted. He needs to do no research; it is I, he says, that needs to read the likes of Jordan Peterson, a man who argues that compulsory marriage is a sound solution to the murder of women by men known as "incels."[16] Yes, I am concerned.

They argue that women, lesbians, gay men, bisexuals, trans, genderqueer, and gender non-conforming people, that Black and Brown people, that immigrants – everyone but them chooses to embrace an identity of victimhood. I have yet to find any person or group who has experienced an identity-based form of harm, harassment, abuse, discrimination who *wants* to be labeled a victim. Those in my profession continue to navigate the complexity of victimhood and survivorhood, even though the word "victim" simply means that something has happened to you. And some people prefer the term "survivor." Why? We blame the victim. We champion survivors. (Aren't you picturing pink boxing gloves right now?) We blame and blame and blame the victim. We rarely blame the perpetrators. Victimhood is seen as weakness and passivity. Yet whose actions are we making invisible here? Men want all the credit for everything they build, and none for any time they cheat and destroy. Just flip through any newspaper and look at the headlines. We talk about those who experience sexual assault, those who experience racism, those who flee their home country. Where's the actor who committed those harms, who engaged in the threatening behavior, who engaged in the deprivation, who disrespected boundaries, dignity, and autonomy? Why do we routinely erase the bad actor? Who is invisible now? Who is passive now?

There is no passivity in victimhood. Victims resist, struggle, fight, endure, persist, heal, learn, advocate, survive and thrive. Action verbs abound. Victims often spend far too much time engaging in self-blame, searching for ways to hold themselves accountable, when the perpetrators run, lie, deny, and use any tools they can to cheat the system (especially money; money pays the lawyers). Accountability, strength, courage, leadership – values still *(still!)* often seen as male (who were you picturing?) are demonstrated every single day by those who have experienced victimization. They embrace their fears and their uncertainty, and they forge ahead. Victims are powerful. The oppressed are powerful. Black women are powerful. Immigrants are powerful. The proof of their power is everywhere. Their actions, their movements, command our attention. They demonstrate assertiveness every day. Whoever you are, dear reader, whatever your identity or life experience thus far, assertiveness belongs to you. You have earned it. Let's not leave it to use only by those who haven't.

PERMISSION OR FORGIVENESS

DATE

LEARN TO ASK FORGIVENESS INSTEAD OF PERMISSION
IDENTIFY 10 TIMES IN YOUR ADULT LIFE WHEN YOU THOUGHT YOU SHOULD DO SOMETHING BUT DID NOT ACT. WHAT STOPPED YOU? DID YOU CONSULT WITH SOMEONE? DO YOU USUALLY MAKE YOUR OWN DECISIONS, OR DO YOU LOOK TO OTHERS TO LEAD? DOES INVOLVING OTHERS MAKE YOU DOUBT YOURSELF?

1.
2.
3.
4.
5.
6.
7.
8.
9.
10.

CHAPTER SEVEN

Your Personal Relationship Rights

"I try my best to confront situations because I know, at the end of the day, you can deal with it or it will deal with you. I've had enough experience to know that that's how it goes down. There's no going around it."

— Jada Pinkett Smith —

Assertiveness is a great tool for building a better relationship with yourself – and with others. How many books are there out there on the importance of communication in relationships? Probably thousands. Communication skills are crucially important, we tend to learn the hard way. We learn too late, sadly, much of the time. And then we perpetuate the problem by failing to teach healthy communication skills to children, generation after generation. This can stop right here, right now, with you. As you have likely noticed, if you find yourself learning something in these pages, I expect you to pay it forward. Surely, parent readers, you want your children to have an easier time than you've had in your relationships (with family, friends, romantic, and otherwise). Assertive communication skills will help you define and maintain boundaries, to establish and convey your personal relationship rights, and with those rights, comes also responsibility.

Why a rights framework? Well, let's start in what is probably an unexpected place – there are plenty of women I do not like. Yes, indeed. Sometimes people marvel that I say that out loud. They seem to mistakenly believe that as a feminist, I am supposed to unconditionally adore all women. I don't. Who does? Instead, when considering the category that is all women, I can readily acknowledge that anyone who has lived as a woman on this planet has experienced some aspect of life that is made difficult by that identity. The range of women's experiences is vast and varied. I advocate for women's rights and advancement, for equity and equality, for their agency and autonomy. And, I think plenty of people are confused about what feminism is because it never meant we couldn't find each other annoying! Hot tip: we all do.

So instead of pretending, politely but inauthentically, that we all want to and should get along (who said?), how about we all learn to coexist while appreciating difference, to respect each other's boundaries and dignity, to engage ethically and transparently? How else will we avoid the strong forces pulling us back into the artificiality of that insincere politeness and faux humility? And it's fake, believe me. But you already know that, don't you?

Generationally, we tend to think differently about humility. Boomers, I'm afraid, have held on tightly to the Miss America or Hitchcock blonde feminine ideals, and better yet if she is beautiful but doesn't know it. Beautiful but doesn't know it. There's even a country song dedicated to this very idea. (My apologies to the Boomers and Gen Xers who will now have that song in your head for the rest of the day. It is a catchy tune.) And what is wrong with that, you ask? Well, let's unpack that nonsense here. Who is the beauty for? Who does it serve? Who benefits from her beauty if she is unaware of it? And isn't that great for him? Rhetorical question. Similarly, how many of you have heard your mother or mother-in-law lament the self-absorption of contemporary (Gen X and Millenial) mothers? Whether self-absorbed, self-centered, narcissistic – pick a word – what they mean is selfish. And let's unpack that nonsense here. What behavior is selfish? Taking time for oneself? Taking a girls' trip? Regularly scheduled exercise? Working? Not working? Having children at a young age and then enjoying the years when the children are grown? Having children at or after 40 after having a successful career but perhaps not being in your athletic prime when your children are adolescents? The impossible damned-if-you-do-or-don't list could go on the entire length of this book. I know this. I've found myself in the middle of these conversations countless times, and I do not even have children! Now dissimilarly, at both feminist academic and activist conferences, participants have riled each other, across the generations, prompting the usual refrain – we just wish younger women would be more grateful. Whew. Okay. I get it. I really do. I'm no longer a young feminist (by actual definition! Some groups define "young feminists" as 30 or 35 and younger.), but I have lived long enough to see how new generations may not have learned feminist history (which is not their fault, in a patriarchy), may not feel deferential and may feel entitled – both goals of feminist movements, actually, regardless of wave. That's right. See, while I personally may not enjoy feeling that my individual efforts are not being appreciated or recognized by those who have come after me (that's the ego at work), I also welcome the audacity with which younger women increasingly engage with the world around them. Wasn't that the point? Isn't it? To feel entitled to equality? We are entitled to our rights; that's what rights are. Now we cannot age ourselves back into believing that women should be seen and not heard. We should not slip back into reinforcing the gender binary inadvertently, either, by insisting that they engage aggressively when fighting men but expect traditional gender norms when interacting with us or other women.

Women, too, can be part and parcel of the patriarchy. We were raised in it, and it is all around us. Patriarchal white supremacy is the water, not the shark, as Kyle "Guante" Tran Myhre so helpfully explains. Plenty of us resist its influence, but uncomfortably and repeatedly find that it keeps creeping back in, if we're telling ourselves the truth. I'm in the middle now, generationally speaking, and I am not trying to contribute to a vicious culture in which feminists (pick any movement, really) eat their own. Instead, I want to remind us that a rights framework may be useful – neither floor nor ceiling but a firm foundation all the same, an anchor or home base to which to return, upon which to reflect before burning out or writing off others.

Entitlement is a problem when it comes to privilege – not rights. Entitlement is what women need to set boundaries. Humility, timidity, restraint, politeness, a gentle nature, and so on does not a safe, healthy woman make. Not in a patriarchy. Not in patriarchal white supremacist governments. Not in, as bell hooks says, in imperialist, white-supremacist, capitalist patriarchy. Look around! Where's the lie? So, yeah, I'll take some entitlement in these young women every damn day. My elder friends – you should, too. I know that you may not think you want to foster these historically unfeminine qualities in the young women and girls around you, but I talk to your daughters and nieces and employees day in and day out and have for over fifteen years now, and sadly, I know many of them better than you ever will. I'm sorry to say it. You think they respect you because they are performing respect for you by not speaking up. They think you respect them because you don't see who they truly are. This mismatch is disastrous. The pursuit of some impossible feminine ideal leaves almost everyone feeling inadequate in some way, and the individual woman often feels as if she is failing herself, her kind, and the other women in her life. These women may mistakenly believe that their personal failures are the cause of their anxiety, depression, abuse, eating disorder, test anxiety, self-harm, sexual insecurities, and more. They seek out counselors, therapists, victim advocates, career coaches, academic advisors, trusted faculty, older or more experienced peers – anyone who will listen and provide counsel! And for many, their mothers and grandmothers cannot be counted upon to provide healthy forms of support. We're getting something wrong here, generation after generation. I'm a lot of women's trusted counsel, second mom, or "like a cool aunt." I hope I am actually the cool aunt, too. But know, too, that the women whose daughters have hugged me and told me or my team members that we have saved or changed their lives often discount what we're trying to tell them when they realize that we do not have our own biological children. I don't say this defensively. I don't work for the parents; that's not my calling. I do the work precisely because I know young people need someone other than parents, and those hugs and comments are satisfying and rewarding and keep people in jobs like mine going. I'm sharing this bluntly here to tell you, if you'll listen, that there is so much about your children that you do not know. But they want you to know! They wish they could reach out to you. But they tell me, time and time again, that their parents and grandparents, whom they love dearly, want them to be a different type of girl. This is heartbreaking, especially because our familial relationships do not have to be this way.

Assertiveness is a lifeboat. Let assertiveness at least be the lifeguard guiding you to shore. Assertiveness in relationships comes out as clearly articulated wants and needs, boundaries set and honored, honest, straightforward, and ethical engagement and interactions with those in relationships with us. These healthy relationship behaviors should be exercised daily, if done well. You (and your children and their grandparents) are entitled – yes, entitled – to this fair treatment. Assertive communication is something we should both give and receive.

In the healthiest of relationships, all involved must engage assertively. Sadly, many of our gender norms and other societal hierarchies routinely get in the way. You must decide what you truly value in each different type of relationship when choosing how to wield your newfound assertiveness skills. For example, what do we really mean by the value of "respecting our elders"? Does that mean we just let grandma say racist things and talk about her later behind her back? Does that mean we teach our children and grandchildren to keep our opinions to ourselves? Do our children know the difference between their opinions, their feelings, and their boundaries? How do they know? Have you taught them? So, if grandma says racist things, and uncle says sexist things, and another uncle doesn't say problematic things but is touchy-feely, and one aunt is just loud, how is the child supposed to behave? Do they know how to navigate the complexity of holiday get-togethers and family reunions? I have questions! But more importantly, I have concerns.

In our romantic relationships, who gets to drive the relationship? Who gets to initiate sexual activity? Who should want sex more? Who should have sex early and often, and who should wait? Why should they wait? How much sex is too much? Too little? Do we owe sex to our spouses? What if we aren't married? Who shouldn't we have sex with, when, where, and why? And how do we learn this? If you're responsible for raising or teaching others, how clear were these conversations? I have questions. I have **concerns**. In a nation with little-to-no, but often abysmal sexual health education, I have many concerns.

What kind of touch is healthy? How many conversations about different types of affection and touch and forms of physical pleasure have you ever had with others? So how are we going to get young people to feel entitled to boundaries, again? You see where I'm going here, I hope. So, yes, I will take some loud, pushy, entitled, opinionated boundary-setting teens and young adults, any day. I'll take some loud, pushy, entitled, opinionated, boundary-setting middle-aged and elderly folks any day, too.

Perhaps you're not yet convinced. Yet the proof is everywhere. The proof is right here, too, and I know that because I am writing yet another book about women and assertiveness, and here you are reading it. And again, like the assertiveness books of yesteryear (peaking in the early 1970s and again in the early-to-mid 1990s), a chapter on relationship rights felt obligatory. We are still working on these aspects of gender equality. And again, to persuade you, dear reader, to continue on this journey we needed to work through some unlearning and undoing before moving forward, so that you, too, may feel entitled to these rights and better able to embrace them as your own. I wish that I could speak directly to women, particularly Gen X and Boomer women, and have them immediately feel entitled to these relationship rights, but that specter of selfishness continually gets in the way. How does that irksome voice incessantly creep back in? The push-and-pull of this journey can be exhausting, I know. The reward for your efforts is that the voice visits less and less often, her volume fades over time, and your consideration of her noise becomes reduced to the time it takes to roll your eyes at whichever woman in your life the voice embodies. Take your pick.

So, at last we've arrived. Here we are. Here we go. You are ENTITLED to the following relationship RIGHTS, including but not limited to:

- You have the right to be physically safe within a relationship
- You have a right to be free from emotional, verbal, and financial abuse within a relationship
- You have the right to share your feelings, wants, and needs in a relationship
- You have the right to prioritize your health and well-being and not sacrifice yourself for the sake of the other(s) or the relationship
- You have the right to balance within a relationship; what you give or put into a relationship should generally be equal to what you get or get out of a relationship
- You have the right to have friendships, acquaintances, social activity and involvement outside of your romantic or sexual relationships
- You have the right to both privacy and alone time
- You have the right to experience sexual desire
- You have the right to reject sexual advances
- You have the right to take steps to ensure your own sexual safety

and reproductive health (e.g., use of condoms, birth control, etc.)
- You have the right to grow and change over the course of the relationship, as does your partner
- You have the right to address a person's behavior if it impacts you (remember, though, that they have the right to choose to change their behavior or not)
- You have the right to leave a situation or relationship that is not good for you
- You have the right to pursue work of your own interest and control your own money
- You have the right to ask for help

Remember, that every person in a relationship (of any kind) has those rights. Healthy and assertive communication works both ways. Ideally. You must keep in mind that you can only control yourself – what you say or don't say and how you respond. So, let's take another look at that same list from another perspective, that of your partner(s):

- They have a right to be physically safe within the relationship; you should not physically harm them
- They have a right to be free from emotional, verbal, and financial abuse within the relationship; you should not inflict such abuse
- They, too, have the right to share their feelings, wants, and needs in a relationship, which you should listen to and consider sincerely
- They, too, have the right to prioritize their own health and well-being and not sacrifice themselves for your sake or the sake of the relationship
- They have the right to balance within a relationship; what they give or put into the relationship should generally be equal to what they get or get out of the relationship
- They have the right to have friendships, acquaintances, social activity and involvement outside of your relationship
- They have the right to both privacy and alone time
- They have the right to experience sexual desire

- They have the right to reject your sexual advances
- They have the right to take steps to ensure their own sexual safety and reproductive health (e.g., use of condoms, birth control, etc.)
- They have the right grow and change over the course of the relationship, even in ways you might not like or prefer
- They have the right to address your behavior if it impacts them
- They have the right to leave a situation or the relationship
- They have the right to pursue work of their own interest and control their own money
- They have the right to ask for help

It is common for those on an assertiveness-building journey to go through a phase (or two) of hyper-assertiveness, in which they are energized and optimistic and exercising their new skills regularly. Be mindful that if you are making up for lost time and feeling done holding yourself back, this new mindset may be startling to your friends and family and romantic/sexual partners. They do not have to be on board. They do not have to ride out your life changes. We hope that they will. We hope they embrace this! But your rights don't trump the rights of others. The healthiest, most egalitarian relationships strive to maintain this balance. Inevitably, life happens, and one person will experience a rough time and need more, for a while, than the other. And then, vice versa. Assertive living does not mean you abandon your partner who needs more from you for a while. All relationships experience this ebb and flow. Good relationships require give and take and some compromise. There's a difference in delaying a conversation about your relationship for a day or two if your partner had a bad day at work or has an important project coming up and in feeling unable to address the issue for months or years because of fear of how they may react. You should continue to be ethical, considerate and compassionate as your exercise your personal relationship rights, but you need not be sacrificial, submissive, or afraid. Those feelings are often red flags, markers of an imbalance. Again, context matters, particularly duration and frequency; explore those feelings and consider talking about this aspect of your relationship with a therapist, counselor, or trusted friend. On your own, you can search online for tools, such as the Emotions Wheel created by American psychologist Dr. Robert Plutchik or one of its many adaptations. This self-examination is time well spent, as many people spend years reacting with a performance of feeling or emotion that is really masking the origin of its expression. What are comfortable emotions for you? Which feelings are uncomfortable? What emotions do you try to mask? Do you lean back into passive-aggressive behavior rather than communicate how you really feel? Engaging assertively means saying what you mean and meaning what you say. Remember, it's a practice. The more you learn about yourself, your feelings, and your reactions to the behavior of others, the more you will be able to think clearly and quickly and control your response. A sample diagram for mapping your feelings is provided on the following page, along with some space to jot down your notes. Feel free to mark this page and flip back to this diagram as is helpful when reflecting upon the feelings that arise as you engage with others assertively.

YOUR PERSONAL RELATIONSHIP RIGHTS

WHAT AM I REALLY FEELING?

Making Sense of our Emotions (and Working Through a Few Lies We Tell Ourselves)

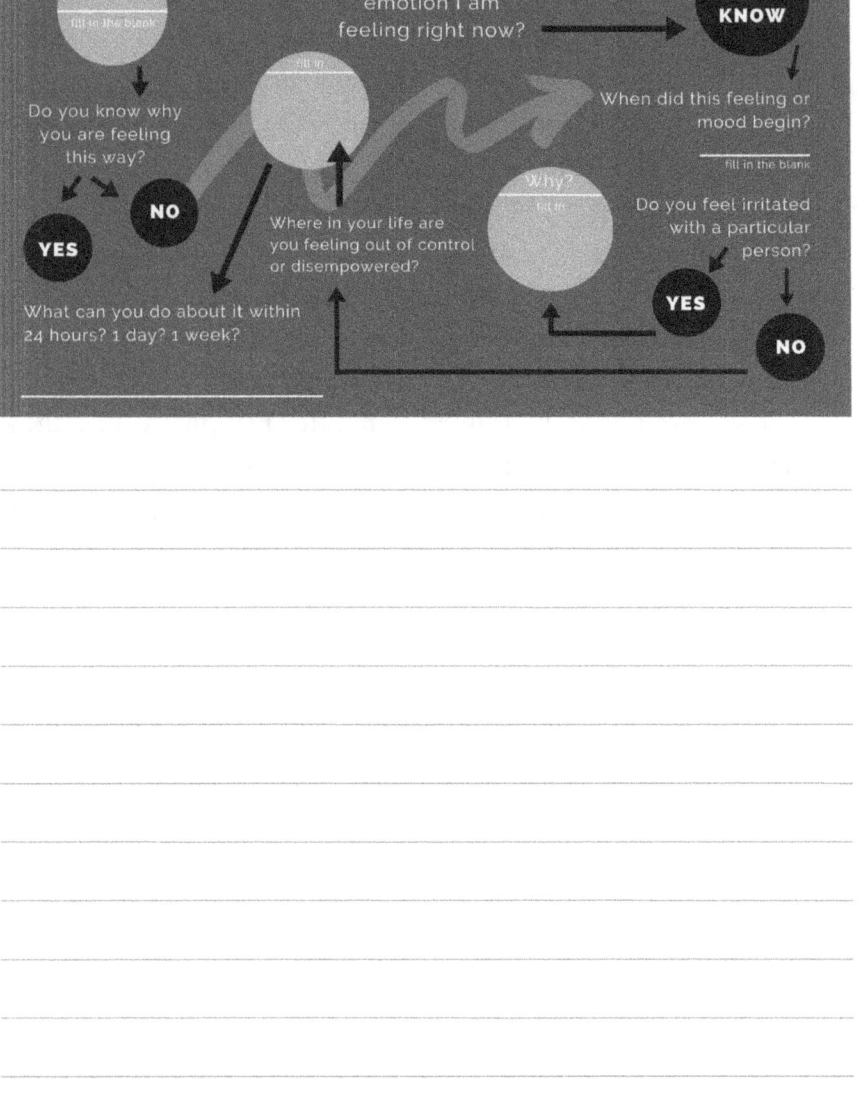

LIST OF WANTS
AN EXERCISE IN SELF-KNOWING

What I Want:

What I Really Want:

What I Really, Really Want:

Did you feel able to unapologetically list your wants (not needs) here? How can we move from thinking about our wants internally to asking out loud for our wants to be met?

CHAPTER EIGHT

Assertiveness at Work

> *"Probably my worst quality is that I get very passionate about what I think is right."*
>
> — Hillary Clinton —

Assertiveness in the workplace should take a variety of forms. Sometimes, assertiveness is necessary for participation and problem-solving; sometimes, assertiveness is required for boundary-setting and self-protection. There are those among us who happily and simply follow orders at work, although those type of employees are likely not reading this book. The rest of us must learn to speak up. Assertiveness at work may be characterized as initiative, problem-solving, a can-do attitude, or described as having strong communication or leadership skills. Sometimes, assertiveness is displayed through one's ability to coordinate and lead a team or in navigating a company's internal politics. Some level of assertiveness is required for success in any of these tasks. Given that our workplaces are not actually meritocracies, we are unable to judge someone's assertiveness by job title alone. You know who I'm talking about – every workplace has some mediocrity in leadership.

If you are reading this book, you surely have ambition. Be ambitious! Admit your ambition. So what? You want to do something productive with your life? You wish to contribute over the many, many, many hours we spend at work over *decades*? Yes! I do. I have always been the most motivated when I have a sense of purpose, even when my job was to assist in bringing about the vision of other leaders. Now I am motivated by my own sense of purpose, execute strategy and have vision, and lead others. The only way to get there successfully is by building assertiveness. Ambition is perhaps the root of assertiveness. Or, perhaps assertiveness waters the roots of ambition. Either way, I'll take both.

Actress and producer Reese Witherspoon has spoken about women's ambition several times over recent years, perhaps most famously at the 2015 Glamour Women of the Year awards ceremony.[17] Her acceptance speech from that night went viral, at least among the professional womens' social media networks and across celebrity news outlets. This clip continues to pop up every now and again, nearly five years later. That night, she asked the audience why ambition is considered a dirty word for women. She mentioned studies that have found that both men and women tend to link women's ambition with negative associations such as self-centeredness or ruthlessness, when we do not do so in our evaluations of men. Ambition is somehow considered a negative personality trait among women candidates for leadership positions, even at companies focused on products designed for women, and significantly (disastrously?) among candidates for political office. I don't know about you, but I want my presidential candidates to be ambitious, to have been ambitious, and to lead ambitiously while in office. We've always admired that in the many, many men who have purportedly represented us, also their constituents, in those governmental roles. Do you feel well represented? Start voting for the ambitious women on the ballot. You need not run for office yourself, although I think you should. At least stop judging the women candidates more harshly than you do the men. Women won't solve everything. Women can be mediocre, harmful, even. But we deserve to be there right alongside the men in this representative republic. We need our so-called "women's issues" to matter, to be enacted and funded. Women's issues are worthy. They benefit over 50% of our population, since women's issues are also family issues. Women's issues are children's issues. Women's issues are health and environmental issues. The label is ridiculous and misleading, and sexism operates to keep those issues and concerns trivialized.

Frankly, readers, it is quite clear that being nice and covertly ambitious isn't getting the job done. Women have not achieved equity anywhere by being nice. Neither women's politeness nor women's ambition have undone the deep sexism permeating our public and private spheres. The sexism is built in. It's entrenched; it's structural. Women's gender identity cuts both ways – if you're too nice, you're not seen as a leader, and if you're emerging as a leader and want to keep leading, you're too ambitious? Well, since it's a trap, I'll choose the only way out that allows my authentic, articulated self to show up. I choose assertiveness.

Weigh in. Take on a task and do it well. Volunteer to lead a project and see it through. Opt in, early and often, instead of waiting for yet another Average Joe to run the meeting, take the podium, and get the credit for the work they so often do not do. Your job early on in a career is to do the work. Try to make yourself a consistently contributing team member. Make yourself useful to your supervisor. Be reliable. You will soon find yourself being asked to do more, when

> "One of the issues I kept saying to my students is you have to learn to interrupt. When you raise your hand at a meeting, by the time they get to you, the point is not germane. So the bottom line is active listening. If you are going to interrupt, you look for opportunities. You have to know what you're talking about."
>
> **MADELEINE ALBRIGHT**

you have earned their trust. You need to be visible and contributing but stay in the appropriate lane. Assertiveness without knowledge or experience can come out as recklessness. Bide your time and focus your energy and initiative on problem-solving and learning your field. As your confidence and sense of belonging grows, the assertiveness you bring to the workplace should evolve. Remember, when you gain traction and influence, bring others with you. That's the deal. If you've read this far, know that this author wishes to instill in the reader this sense of obligation. The words of activist Marian Wright Edelman are instructive: "I was taught that the world had a lot of problems; that I could struggle and change them; that intellectual and material gifts brought the privilege and responsibility of sharing with others less fortunate; and that service is the rent each of us pays for living the very purpose of life and not something you do in your spare time or after you have reached your personal goals."

Ambition need not be tied to selfish aims. Ambition is not a dirty word. Sure, you say. You know it's not, you tell me. So, if I ask you to tell someone this week that you are ambitious, that should feel easy. If not, you need to do it. Say it out loud. Say it with me, "I am ambitious." Say it again. Identify your ambition role models. This may feel easy to Gen Xers – we have Madonna and her "Blonde Ambition." (She's worthy of an entire course on ambition and assertiveness, no doubt!) Seventies and Eighties babies enjoyed television heroines Claire Huxtable and Susanna Sugarbaker. We have witnessed the long and storied career of Hillary Rodham Clinton. These women were models for me growing up of standing up, speaking up, of endurance, resilience, and just nerve.

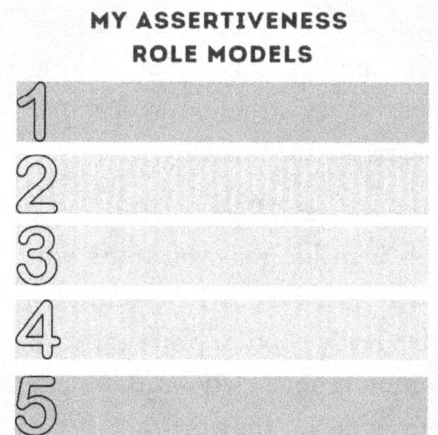

MY ASSERTIVENESS ROLE MODELS
1.
2.
3.
4.
5.

Take a few minutes to consider your early assertive influences and jot down 5 ambition possibility models in the space provided.

I would not be surprised if some of you listed Miss *Legally Blonde* herself, Reese Witherspoon. She acts less and leads more these days. She speaks out. You may have noticed an increasing number of women celebrities, especially those in or past their forties, speaking out these days. As I look around my own far less famous friend group, Gloria Steinem's quote, "Women may be the one group that grows more radical with age," rings true. As Reese Witherspoon closed her now-famous Glamour Women of the Year remarks, she said:

> "I think we are in a culture crisis in every field. In every industry, women are underrepresented and underpaid in leadership positions. Under 5 percent of CEOs of fortune 500 companies are women. Only 19 percent of Congress is women. No wonder we don't have the health care we deserve or paid family leave or public access to early childhood education. That really worries me. How can we expect legislation or our needs to be served if we don't have equal representation? So here's my hope: If you're in politics, media, the tech industry, or working as an entrepreneur or a teacher or a construction worker or a caregiver, you know the problems we are all facing.
>
> I urge each one of you to ask yourselves: What do we do now? That's a big question. What is it in life that you think you can't accomplish? Or what is it that people have said that you cannot do? Wouldn't it feel really good to prove them all wrong? Because I believe ambition is not a dirty word. It's just believing in yourself and your abilities. Imagine this: What would happen if we were all brave enough to be a little bit more ambitious? I think the world would change."

I couldn't have said it better myself. Amen, sister.

Confronting Sexual Harassment at Work

As discussed in Chapter 5, assertiveness may take the form of bystander intervention, which, in the workplace setting, should improve our workplace cultures and bring about more equitable, discrimination-free environments. Thankfully, the confidence we build in standing up for others can also help us learn how to tap into assertiveness in order to stand up for ourselves. Even assertive women sometimes find themselves hesitant to assert themselves in uncomfortable situations. Assertiveness can help nip bad behavior in the bud and send the message that you are not interested or likely to be susceptible to any intended harassment or abuse of power. You must realize, however, that some predators and perpetrators have no intention of hearing or honoring your resistance. No amount of assertiveness in women will, on its own, eliminate sexual violence. Rather, some attempts may be discouraged or thwarted, and we have no business judging or blaming those who have been harmed for what they have experienced at the hands of another person. The perpetrators deserve that judgment and blame. Assertiveness, here, should not be considered a cure, and the lack of assertiveness displayed by a target during an encounter, should never be considered a failure on their part to prevent their own harassment or assault. That's not how this works. Fault and blame lie only with those who harm. Assertiveness training **might** help **sometimes**, and it is impossible to predict which situation you may encounter. That's true for all of us, despite the comfort we may unintentionally take from speculation and victim-blaming that is all too common in our culture.

For those situations for which deterrence may be possible, based upon hearing countless stories of sexual harassment and assault, the following tactics appear to have been useful in certain situations:

Direct Resistance

- State your resistance firmly and directly:

    - "This is making me uncomfortable."
    - "I am not interested in _____."
    - "No."
    - "I do not want to do this."
    - "Stop."

- Leave. If someone has behaved badly toward you, you do not owe them an explanation. Leaving, with or without explanation, sends a strong signal that they have crossed a line.
- Summon a friend, employee of the establishment, coworker, or bystander.

While I wish that these verbal and visible signs of resistance were always sufficient at stopping or preventing harassment and assault, keep in mind that many people continue to believe that persistence is acceptable when initiating sexual activity, and some perpetrators went into the interaction with no intention of honoring your initial attempts to resist. Sadly, the verbal resistance may prove most useful after the encounter, if you choose to report the incident to your school, workplace, or to the police. Although many policies and laws no longer require a victim to have uttered a verbal "no," in routine practice, victim statements that include clearly, firmly stated words of resistance are considered more persuasive, credible, and convincing to friends, family, investigators, and juries alike. I wish the general public had a fuller understanding of how these incidents occur and the wide range of justified human responses to unwanted advances and assault, but I know that much work remains before we will successfully convince everyone to start by believing.

Indirect Resistance

- Fake a phone call. You may politely excuse yourself to take the call. Upon your return, you may apologize, if you find that most comfortable or persuasive, and tell the person that you have to leave. You probably do not need to go into detail here with an excuse, but "family emergency," often works well, particularly if you have children, as a societally acceptable or justifiable excuse.
- Say you are not feeling well. Excuse yourself, maybe conveying a sense of urgency, if you are worried your quick departure may come across as rude.
- Excuse yourself to go to the restroom. If you are a woman and the person making you uncomfortable is a man, remember that men are often somewhat uncomfortable or uninformed about women's bodies, and almost all of us have been taught that questioning bodily functions and bathroom habits is considered rude behavior and a violation of reasonable expectations of personal privacy.
- Create a buddy system with your best friend or group of friends. Have a code word that you can text them to prompt a call, or have a friend who knows where you are going to be, if, say, it's a date, happy hour, or meeting where a potential harasser may be, to call 45 minutes after you've arrived. Consider the nature of the activity. Getting that call or text too early may not be useful, as many perpetrators intentionally display friendly, charming, hospitable behavior at the outset, to encourage targets to let down their guard.
- Act as if you see someone you know and excuse yourself to go say hello to them. It is not actually necessary that you know the person. That may feel strange, but there is usually some camaraderie among humankind out there you can tap into. At worse, play it off as a mistake, saying, "Oh! I'm sorry, I thought you were somebody else," if you have to. I suggest finding a friendly-looking face, maybe someone who shares some aspect of identity with

you, and approach them as if you know them and say, "Hi! I know this is odd, but can you please act as if you know me, so I can extricate myself from an uncomfortable situation?" Chances are they will say yes. Consider a group of intoxicated women in a bathroom, whether at a bar or a wedding – women know what it is like to be women, and sometimes we beautifully lean in to help each other out.

- Spill your drink. This creates a distraction that will disrupt the moment and necessitate a response. If you spill something upon yourself, you'll be able to excuse yourself to the restroom. Make enough of a mess, and you'll have an excuse to go home or back to your hotel room to change. If you can, be considerate. For example, in a movie theater, it may be better to spill popcorn than a soft drink, in terms of the mess it makes and the work it creates for someone else to clean up; however, your safety is paramount, and I, for one, want you to do what you need to do to keep yourself safe.

A Note on Work Events Involving Potential Perpetrators

Based upon my experience working with college students, faculty, and staff, I want to strongly recommend that you do what you can to avoid accepting a ride home from or with the person making you uncomfortable. Trust your instincts. Avoid, as much as you are able, their efforts to further get you alone. If you are at a conference or other out-of-town work activity, try to avoid getting into the elevator at the same time at the end of the evening to go to your respective rooms. I repeatedly hear about many uncomfortable situations that arise in these particular moments, which can be readily used as opportunity by those intending to make unreciprocated, unwanted sexual advances. Go so far as to get on the elevator with them, if you think you must, and then act surprised at the last second, as if you forgot something, and say you are going to grab something at the hotel convenience shop or front desk, and call out, "See you tomorrow!"

Advice for Interacting with the Overly Cautious Non-Harasser

In this situation, your assertiveness will need to take a different shape. If you have noticed changed behavior among men in your workplace, such as leaving the office door open, no longer inviting you to lunches, dinners, happy hours, or recreational activities for networking, or to travel with them on business trips, if that was routine before, or even in holding one-on-one meetings with women who report to them, you may benefit from alleviating their new, if reactionary, concerns directly. Depending upon your pre-existing relationship with this person, some of you may be able to pointedly ask, "Has #MeToo[18] made you worry about how you are interacting with the women at work?" Realize that asking this question may prompt a fearful, "Why do you ask?" in response, so be prepared to follow up with specific examples, if you take this approach, to explain why you're asking. Realize, that if worried, the person may be concerned that they have done something wrong, even if they haven't. (Realize, also, that someone you feel safe with could be harassing or harming someone else and wonder if you have heard about it.) Most people may not wish to approach the conversation this directly, for a variety of reasons. Without specifically stating that you are trying to counter #MeToo's unintended consequences, proactively request the one-on-one time with your mentor, supervisor, or helpfully experienced or connected colleague. Ease them back into a comfortable working relationship. Start with meeting in the workplace or in public. Start with meeting for coffee, instead of asking the fearful person to a place likely to have you or them ordering alcoholic drinks. Start with breakfast or a snack break, then lunch, and then dinner. If you need to have a closed-door meeting, be the one who closes the door. However, if you do not actually need the door closed, I do recommend we begin embracing more open doors, to help protect others. Let some light in – we don't always know who needs protecting. We also cannot predict when we may want witnesses or a quick exit, so let's begin erring on the side of open doors, daylight, and crowds, for a more open environment.

ASSERTIVENESS AT WORK

DATE:

STRENGTH IN NUMBERS
IDENTIFY 6 VALUES, QUALITIES, OR SKILLS THAT MAKE YOU FEEL STRONG, CAPABLE, AND WORTHY OF THE LIFE YOU WANT

CHAPTER NINE

Raise Hell and Raise Angry Girls

*"Anger has a bad rap, but it is actually one of the most hopeful
and forward thinking of all our emotions.
It begets transformation, manifesting our passion
and keeping us invested in the world.
It is a rational and emotional response to trespass,
violation, and moral disorder. It bridges the divide between
what 'is' and what 'ought' to be, between a difficult past
and an improved possibility."*

— Soraya Chemaly —

We need not only to tap into our own anger, we must also begin to instill it in our daughters. This chapter is not only for mothers, but for aunts, teachers, coaches, student affairs professionals, supervisors, mentors, grandmothers – everyone. Research tells us that women often feel better with age, feeling more content, confident, authentic, settled, stronger, independent, you name it, at forty (or so) than they did at twenty. I know that I have no desire to go back to my twenties. No, thank you. What is it that is so freeing about getting older for women? So many of us will say, thankfully, that we care so much less about what people think of us. We keep it moving. We know who we are, and we have found our people. We know this mentality or life phase is healthier and happier – we're living it – yet we keep perpetuating the cycle by socializing girls to keep on caring. That's how patriarchy works, and this is one of the roles we play in it – until we choose to break the cycle.

As mentioned, my career has been focused on women's empowerment and equity, and most recently I have focused particularly on addressing sexual harassment and assault on a college campus. In addition to working with thousands of college students, I talk to my fair share of parents, who are often quite involved in their young adult children's lives these days. They ask me, "What can I do?" and they mean, "How can I help my child reduce their own risk of experiencing sexual assault?" At this point, I've narrowed in on two primary recommendations:

1 The United States is in desperate need of earlier, accurate, comprehensive sex education in its K-12 schools; and
2 We must allow our children to feel and express anger.

Granted, for the parent of a first-year college student, this advice may come too late. I am sharing it now in hopes that it is not too late for the young people in your life – and not just the girls. People, and young people in particular, need to be allowed to feel and express anger, and the rest of us should not be so afraid of it. Yes, there is a time and place for good manners. That is not what I am discouraging. But many parents err too far away from the side of safety, raising children so well-behaved that they learn to suffer in silence, so protected that they do not recognize the threat of danger, so ignorant and ashamed of their bodies and sexuality that they turn anywhere but to their guardians for help when navigating young adulthood and when experiencing trauma. I know this for sure because I talk to your children. Or rather, your children talk to me and to countless other victim advocates and health and wellbeing counselors worldwide, when they feel unable to talk to you. Sometimes, instead of feeling thankful that the child found help that they needed, parents project their feelings of hurt and inadequacy back onto the injured child in dismay. "Why didn't you talk to me?!" Often, that is just the first of many questions posed to them that begins with "Why didn't you…" And there's your answer.

When sexual harassment and sexual assault remain rampant in our country, we are not getting prevention right. Neither parents nor schools are balancing expectations of good child/student behavior with allowances for justified outrage and righteous indignation. When #MeToo goes viral overnight, with thousands of daughters sharing that they, too, have experienced this gendered, sexist, misogynistic abuse everywhere – from the halls of Congress to your local small-town church, we must grapple with the harsh reality that we are getting it *really* wrong. Sexual harassment prevention should not be a **trend** in higher education and the workplace, yet here we are, again, 30 years after it was all the rage in the early 1990s. Anita Hill gave a masterclass in all of this to the nation back in 1992, and here we still are. Women cannot keep living through these harms, acknowledging our shared experiences and finding much-needed solidarity, yet continue to raise surprised, unprepared daughters. You know who is not burying their heads in the sand? Feminist moms. Progressive dads. Parents of Black and Brown children. Trans and gender non-binary parents and caregivers. They raise healthy kids every day, kids who may, due to discrimination faced by their parents and guardians, lack much of the privilege had by so many of their majority white heterosexual, cisgender counterparts, people who may very well deny such privilege while striving to create a childhood so comfortable for their children that they remain reluctant to address the world's brutality, in hopes of delaying the inevitable, but leaving the children woefully unprepared for the harms that may come their way.

If I have pissed some of you off, well, that is kind of the point. To be comfortable with anger in our children, we must get comfortable with the feeling in ourselves. The underside of this longing for pleasantries, politeness, respectability, and comfort at all times is the idea that anger is bad and unhealthy. Anger at a violation is not problematic. Anger when violated is a should. Anger at injustice is very healthy. We could use more of that, please. Anger for me, is fuel, and it drives me to action. That feeling is transformative. That quick shift from anger to action is the internal processing our most vulnerable needs right now. Not only are we not teaching this resistance – we are actively discouraging it! This kind of anger may be what your child needs most for self-protection. This anger is what many of us needed and found far too late. I appreciate good manners almost as much as I appreciate the Oxford comma, but I know that both have their time, place, and limitations.

Anger, like assertiveness, will not solve everything. Yet when I am asked what do I need most to tackle the issue I am asked to address every day, this is where I land. Anger and assertiveness are linked and should not be thought of as mutually exclusive. Anger is not the same as aggressiveness. Plenty of anger is justified. Plenty of anger can be healthy. Anger can get you out of bed in the morning. Anger can motivate you to charge into battle.

From my own childhood, there are moments that stick out, that in retrospect, surprise me about my parents and make me appreciate them for letting me be me. My mother and my beloved piano teacher Mrs. Beasley both let me, without protest, perform quite angry, pounding piano solos at recitals for years when I was in elementary school and a new learner. I cannot imagine that was pleasurable for anyone involved, as I spent ample time practicing on the piano in the living room of our small family home. My twin sister regularly chose softer, prettier pieces, which I am sure both my mother and Mrs. Beasley preferred. Tara and I would go to these recitals, often in matching dresses, always with our rhyming names, of course. So I'd go up to the piano in my frilly dress, tights, and favorite patent Mary Janes, and proceed to sit down and play songs about battles and drama, before advancing to Beethoven (arguably the Metallica of his era). Thankfully, during my teen years, I shifted toward Chopin and Debussy and learned other ways to convey feeling and proficiency, yet I delight now in the memory of those early recitals. One time, I started off on the wrong notes and proceeded to pound away 2 notes off for the entire war dance number I had chosen that year. Afterwards, my parents were amused. Mrs. Beasley appreciated my show-must-go-on determination. I was not scolded or shamed. I did not have to be appropriate or ladylike or perfect. I had made a mistake and carried on unwounded. I did not learn to hate piano and fear performance. This was a healthy, formative childhood experience, and we can all laugh about it today. Make sure your children have those moments and spaces in their young lives.

Similarly, I'm delighted to share, Former First Lady Michelle Obama opens her own memoir, *Becoming*, with her own childhood story of piano lessons and resistance – committing the crime of skipping ahead in her lessons book. She describes her more "freewheeling" approach to her instructor's methods, and her stubborn but determined nature; she continued practicing and improving, all the while challenging the regimented regimen. Obama concludes this anecdote by saying, "I think my parents appreciated my feistiness and I'm glad for it. It was a flame inside me they wanted to keep lit."[19] This, from the three-time winner of Most Admired Woman in America.[20]

The woman who ranked second to Michelle Obama as Most Admired Woman in America in 2020, Kamala Harris, also shares stories of girlhood stubbornness and independence in her memoir, *The Truths We Hold: An American Journey*. Her parents intentionally exposed her to their activist efforts very early on; in fact, Kamala and her sister attended marches and organizing meetings, and chanted alongside them. Harris's childhood in California as a Black, Asian American daughter of immigrant parents, then as a child of divorced hard-working parents, coupled with time spent in the community cultural center Rainbow Sign more than explain her life thus far of hard work, determination, and strength. She too, describes parental influences of high expectations paired with encouragement for her, as a little girl, to run free. Free from rigid gender norms, her father encouraged her to run outside, and she writes that she "would take off, the wind in my face, with the feeling that I could do anything."[21] Undoubtedly, the way she was raised – the early exposure to injustice and citizen protest, the promise of the transformational power of education and an instilled work ethic, and the encouragement to run fast and free – serves as the strong foundation of her impressive legal and political career. Bold but not brash, Harris has a long-documented history of standing up for others. As a former law student myself, I marveled at one early act of independence she discusses in her book, in which she quickly sprang into action as a law student/intern to ensure that an innocent bystander who had been arrested during a large drug bust was discharged on a Friday afternoon, rather than spend a weekend in jail. Student. Intern. Friday afternoon. These are not the most promising conditions for addressing injustice! Undaunted, Harris describes her immediate preoccupation with the potentially snowballing negative effects the arrest and jailtime could have on this woman, and she rushed to plead with the clerk of the court. Because someone (Harris) noticed and cared, stood up and spoke out, the woman was able to come before the judge at the end of that business day and was freed and able to go home to her children. Harris writes, "It was a defining moment in my life. It was the crystallization of how, even on the margins of the criminal justice system, the stakes were extraordinarily high and intensely human. It was a realization that, even with the limited authority of an intern, people who cared could do justice." [22]Now, that's what I would want my child to do, wouldn't you? That's the type of person I still strive to be.

When we bother to look into the earlier years of our most famous American women, we find story after story of bravery, initiative, and assertiveness. Long before she sat down on the bus, Rosa Parks was an investigator of race-based sexual assaults for the NAACP. Hillary Clinton's childhood and adolescence are replete with examples of early initiative and leadership skills, from being elected in elementary school to the safety patrol, in high school being nominated to her school's Cultural Values Committee, and serving as the senior class president as an undergraduate student at Wellesley College.[23] If you're a Gen Xer or Boomer, you likely grew up learning about Sacajawea and Pocahontas, two remarkable Native American women who demonstrated bravery, resourcefulness, and autonomy, as their lives were brought into connection and conflict with American colonialism.[24] Teach the children in your lives about Loujain al-Hathloul, a Saudi women's rights activist who defied Saudi Arabia's ban on women driving, leading to the repeal of that law. Although the law was repealed, Loujain al-Hathloul remains a political prisoner at this time. Activists around the globe continue to advocate for her and protest the arrest, conviction, and detainment conditions and treatment. Likely better known to white American parents and children is Malala Yousafzai, who began her activism as a young child when she wrote a blog post for the BBC describing the inadequate conditions of the educational system in Pakistan and the inequity women and girls faced in seeking access to education. She argued that it was essential for young women to go to school and gained recognition as a leading voice in this fight for equality. In October of 2012, the Taliban attempted to assassinate her for this activism, as they felt increasingly threatened by her influence.

As college students, Annie Clark and Andrea Pino grew into their activism and leadership, connecting and then fighting after each had experienced sexual assault and sought assistance from their campus administrators. Like many survivors of sexual assault, they followed the process, reporting the incident to the proper authorities, recounting their experience time and time again, following up on their investigations when transparency and follow-through appeared to be lacking. They didn't seek out this fight; it found them. As in the heyday of the

> "I love to see a young girl go out and grab the world by the lapels. Life's a bitch. You've got to go out and kick ass."
>
> **MAYA ANGELOU**

70s-era Women's Movement, the women met, shared their story, and discovered they were not alone. Clark and Pino eventually met with hundreds of survivors nationwide and then members of Congress and national media. Their initiative, grit, and determination, first to pursue the justice so often promised to victim/survivors in this country, then to pursue justice on behalf of others, started an avalanche of reporting, protest, and change. They were not alone. Young women such as Kamilah Willingham, Kori Cioca, Erica Kinsman, and Emma Sulkowicz gained national attention, intense scrutiny, and harassment for speaking out when they found justice denied. They, too, began quietly, following the reporting procedures of their respective schools or military unit. Ask anyone who works in campus-based victim advocacy, Title IX compliance, or prevention education – these women brought much-needed and long-overdue attention to this issue, a public health crisis impacting educational equity, which lead to additional staff, resources, revised policies and procedures, and scrutiny from the oversight bodies that is necessary to keep institutions' motivations in check. The schools were not sufficiently tackling campus sexual assault prior to this student activism. Higher education has its share of feminist faculty and staff who have long advocated for change around this issue, although few institutions prioritized solutions until the noise and scrutiny driven by these young activists became impossible to deny.

In 2013, three Black women – Alicia Garza, Patrisse Cullors, and Opal Tometi – created #BlackLivesMatter, in response to the acquittal of Trayvon Martin's murderer, George Zimmerman.[25] In 2014, when Mike Brown was killed by a Ferguson police officer, the movement's popularity and influence grew exponentially. Now in its 7th year, the #BlackLivesMatter movement is a global network with over 40 chapters. You've heard of it, no doubt, and they continue to demand answers and create change in their pursuit of justice. Young Black adults and children have always been leaders in movements. Our textbooks forget (or have erased) the participation of Black children in the Civil Rights Movement, who were often on the front lines and experienced the same horrific violence (beatings by law enforcement, the force of a high-pressure water hose, attacks by dogs, arrests, and murder) as the older marchers and protestors faced.[26] In fact, this is what it took, for white people to see the television footage and photographs of children enduring this violence, for many to be convinced that the horrors of racism were real and that something had to change.

We cannot continue to raise children according to rigid gender norms and exaggerated, outdated fantasy versions of femininity (whose fantasy is it, really?), perpetuating harmful gender stereotypes, and then be surprised when they conform to the same ol' gender norms later in life. Women in heterosexual relationships complain that their husbands and boyfriends do not help them around the house, yet they do not teach or expect their sons to do those tasks. Women are living the forty plus years of benefit of a women's movement, while still being expected to be good little girls, pleasant, polite, home chefs, amazing moms, amazing working professionals, look young for their age, be ridiculously thin, and so on. Lead here but not there. Too much and not enough at the same time. Enough with this gendered imposition of shame and perfectionism.

Most likely, the admired adults you hope your children grow up to be likely had such "strong will" or an "independent streak" peek out when they were younger. Sometimes we call them bossy (if women); often, they emerge as leaders. Young people are increasingly changing the world. Young activists that are now household names include Malala Yousafzai, Greta Thunberg, Emma Gonzalez, David Hogg, Alex Wind, Jaclyn Corin, Cameron Kasky, and survivors of the Marjory Stoneman school shooting, Amandla Stenberg, Zendaya, Gavin Grimm, Jazz Jennings, Chanel Miller, and recently, college student athlete Sarah Fuller, who said yes, just days after winning the SEC Tournament title as a member of Vanderbilt's women's soccer team, to joining Vanderbilt's football team. Sarah Fuller was the first woman to play and score in Power Five conference football game. She received overwhelming national attention and support from women, including tweets from Hillary Clinton, Megan Rapinoe, and Billie Jean King. The second football she kicked in a game now resides in the College Football Hall of Fame. She said yes to opportunity and embraced the new, unexpected challenge with enthusiasm. In the many, many interviews she has now given, Fuller credits her parents for supporting her. Please be the parent that cheers your child on, the parent of children who know you have their back. Give them freedom and encouragement to run free. Delight in their early displays of disagreement and independence. Know that a little anger can go a long way when it is fostered instead of repressed – all the way to the White House, and soon, all the way to the Moon.[27]

CHAPTER TEN

Collective Assertiveness and Responsibility

> *"Women have learned to flex their political muscles. You got to flex that muscle to get what you want."*
>
> — Shirley Chisholm —

Enough. Enough already! You've made it this far into the book, so it is clear that a sincere desire for change exists within you. There is nothing left to do but do it. Action is required. Practice makes perfect. I believe in assertive, unapologetic living, and so here's the coaching pep talk message of tough love: there is no half-assing it. Half-assing, by definition, is not assertive. YOU need yourself to step up. Your friends and family need you. Look around – our communities clearly need folks to step up. What I found missing in assertiveness resources when I was on my own skills-building journey was this sense of collective assertiveness – the idea of applying individual assertiveness skill-building to activist organizing and community change. We cannot continue to focus solely on individual development. As Angela Davis has said, "You see, we think individualistically, and we assume that only heroic individuals can make history." I have not encountered an activist, past or present, who does not worry about American individualism and our current manifestation of capitalism and how it distracts us from considering our collective wellbeing. So, I want to remind you – you do not have to go it alone! We know there is strength in numbers. Engaging collectively, rather than simply individually, sustains our momentum and bolsters our courage. Engaging collectively makes us harder to ignore. Engaging collectively guides our individual efforts into generating systemic change.

Lives are literally at stake. Believing passionately is not enough. Seek out growth and sit in discomfort. Live the positive affirmation posts that you like and share on social media. Follow up the private, individual act of reading books like this with more learning and, more importantly, outward directed action. Assertive living cannot occur if you do not put your voice and your body out there, in your home, your workplace, among your friends and family, and into the streets of our communities. Ideal next steps could include enrolling in an empowerment self-defense class, bystander intervention training, anti-racist education workshops, attending your first public vigil or protest, signing or drafting a petition, attending and participating in a local council meeting, or even running for office. We need you!

Chances are you have a friend who sits near you on a scale of assertiveness. Talk with this friend about serving as assertiveness accountability partners for each other and set weekly challenges or goals. Share your successes and process any hesitations or failures. And know that there will be failures. Failed attempts are okay! As a student of assertiveness, know that you can earn partial credit on this homework assignment. To be human is to be imperfect. To be imperfect is to be human. Say that out loud if you need to. (Really, you will benefit from reading those two sentences out loud at least three times.)

If you also struggle with perfectionism and that plays into your fears about assertive living, seek out resources to better understand and help reduce that type of immobilization. Assertive living is in the trying, the getting back up, continuing the conversation, and the making of tough choices.

Once you have cultivated your own assertiveness skills, it is then your responsibility to advocate for others. If you have benefitted from this book, pay it forward. There's so much work to do! Recent years have been rough for us in so many ways. 2020 will live in infamy, and it became infamous by its third month! American individualism is at root of so many of 2020's ills and horrors. Since, as Angela Davis tells us, "Freedom is a constant struggle," collective assertiveness, acts of bystander intervention by the masses, offers our best hope for the future. Voting is an example of an individual act that may be used to both advance self-interest and the rights of others. Of course, voting can be used to advance self-interest at the expense of others. Assertive living means

> "Any time women come together with a collective intention, it's a powerful thing. Whether it's sitting down making a quilt, in a kitchen preparing a meal, in a club reading the same book, or around the table playing cards, or planning a birthday party, when women come together with a collective intention, magic happens."
>
> **PHYLICIA RASHAD**

we seek the AND, not the OR. Voting is an individual action that culminates into the people's power. Admittedly, recent political campaign cycles have been some of the nastiest in history. Divisive partisan politics may continue for the foreseeable future. Show up anyway. Assertive living means showing up for these meaningful, crucial conversations – engaging as individuals with other individuals for collective evolution. White women, in particular, must move past listening and learning and reading on their own and must engage more broadly than the occasional book club or other social gathering, if those groups look, and sound, and live like them. Individual learning, *especially* when the topics are diversity and inclusion, will reach its limits. We must do more, and we must do better. We must collaborate to improve our collective futures.

Let's consider another example, the life circumstance that often attracts women to assertiveness training – the need to negotiate your salary for the first time. How much good does it do to have made this effort if your investment remains limited to a single act of salary negotiation? Maybe you got yourself a raise. And kudos! You deserve it. But that individual act on its own makes for insufficient feminism or activism. Many an employer would love to simply pay you a little bit more while continuing to underpay everyone else. The individual action does not, and the evidence is clear on this, snowball into collective change. Raising one woman's salary makes a tiny dent in pay inequity, sure, but if you stop there, at yourself, and fail to lift others up, how sincere is your dedication to women's issues? Assertiveness is transferable. Assertive living becomes activist and community oriented, contributing to the greater good when harnessed for just causes. During a conversation with Krystal Clark, the creator of S.A.I.L (Success, Authenticity, Innovation, and Love), a series of personal development workshops for women, she labeled this "transferable assertiveness," a term that stuck with me.[28] Transferable assertiveness is the only way to effectively use assertiveness to further equity. So, to transfer the assertiveness skills of salary negotiation, consider being transparent, where appropriate, about your salary with others who might benefit from that information because they, too, face inequity, and mentor others as they work to develop assertiveness skills to negotiate their salaries. Back to the snowball idea – to build a snowman, you've got to keep the ball rolling. The power of assertiveness grows exponentially when engaged in collectively. The benefits of assertive action multiply when assertiveness is utilized communally. From today forward, let's make sure that collective assertiveness remains part of the assertiveness discussion.

Do the work and embrace every opportunity for laughter along the way. Celebrate both your attempts and successes. There is no way

COLLECTIVE ASSERTIVENESS AND RESPONSIBILITY

forward but to try and try again. Know, though, that building an assertive living framework and living the rest of your life assertively is so, so worth the effort. Your future self will thank you. You have made it this far, working through the exercises and enduring messages of tough love, so finish with a commitment to waste no more time drowning in timidity. You are learning to swim and gaining strength for rough waters. I hope you've found this book a useful buoy. But do choose to jump on in; the water is fine.

Acknowledgments

This book would not exist without the unflagging support of my friends and colleagues, notably Sarah Jordan Welch, LaWanda Swan, Sirajah Raheem, Sarah Watson, and Kristin Torrey. Fellow activist sister-friend Becca Tieder has buoyed my spirits in recent years and encouraged me to live untamed and to infuse work with joy and laughter. Truly, there is no other way. Liz Delgado-Fitzgerald of ASSERT Empowerment Self-Defense is a wonderful new addition to my circle of friends, and she models assertive living in a different but so complementary way to how I was initially envisioning this book, and I know our serendipitous crossing of paths has shaped this writing for the better. Plus, she taught me to break boards, which is such a thrilling, confidence-boosting act – I'm forever changed! Thank you, as well, to Linda Ellis Eastman, for our year of uplifting writer's accountability meetings and the benefits of a shared vision for what this book might be. My twin sister Tara Tuttle is my lifelong best friend, frequent collaborator, and relentless supporter. Many of the personal experiences shared here reflect our shared upbringing, and I appreciate Tara's willingness to let me speak so unflinchingly about our lives. Thank you to my mother Carol West Tuttle, who raised me and my siblings to value education and who provided an impressive example of a lifelong career of advocating for others, which her children each carry on, in our respective roles and fields. Thank you to my brother, Marcus Tuttle, for loving his feminist sisters unconditionally as our lives continue to stretch the miles between us. To my dear husband, Lance Bell – thank you for always being in my corner, for always listening, for bringing me coffee, and for being a constant supportive partner who recognizes the value of my work – of women's work – and helps make it possible. And, finally, all my love to Leo and Potus, my beautiful, hilarious, loving pet children. You bring me joy and comfort every day and have made me a better person. Thank you.

Notes

1. Polite. Adjective. Showing or characterized by correct social usage; marked by an appearance of consideration, tact, deference, or courtesy; marked by a lack of roughness or crudities. Available online at *https://www.merriam-webster.com/dictionary/polite* (last accessed 10/25/2020).
2. Cortina LM, Kabat-Farr D, Leskinen EA, Huerta M, Magley VJ. Se-lective Incivility as Modern Discrimination in Organizations: Evidence and Impact. *Journal of Management*. 2013;39(6):1579-1605. doi:10.1177/0149206311418835
3. Gabriel, A. S., Butts, M. M., Yuan, Z., Rosen, R. L., & Sliter, M. T. (2018). Further understanding incivility in the workplace: The effects of gender, agency, and communion. *Journal of Applied Psychology*, 103(4), 362–382.
4. Philpott, Mary Laura. I *Miss You When I Blink*, Atria Books, Simon & Schuster (2019).
5. Morris, Diana. *The Clarity Workbook*. (2020). Learn more at *www.dianamorris.com*.
6. Naval Adm. William H. McRaven, "Make Your Bed: Little Things That Can Change Your Life...And Maybe the World," speech given May 17, 2014, *https://news.utexas.edu/2014/05/16/mcraven-urges-graduates-to-find-courage-to-change-the-world/*; book of same title, Grand Central Publishing (2017).
7. Jonice Webb, *Running On Empty: Overcome Childhood Emotional Neglect*, Morgan James Publishing; n (October 1, 2012).

8 Bessel van der Kolk, M.D. *The Body Keeps the Score: Brain, Mind and Body in the Healing of Trauma*, Penguin Publishing Group (2014).

9 Consider these visual representations of empathy mapping: David Bland, "Agile Coaching Tip: What Is an Empathy Map?," Accenture SolutionsIQ Blog (2016), available online at *https://www.solutionsiq.com/resource/blog-post/what-is-an-empathy-map/* and Sarah Gibbons, "Empathy Mapping: The First Step in Design Thinking," Nielsen Norman Group (2018), available online at *https://www.nngroup.com/articles/empathy-mapping/*.

10 Margaret Quinn Rosenzweig, "Breaking Bad News: A Guide for Ef-fective and Empathetic Communication," *Nurse Practitioner* (2012), 37(2), pages1-4. doi:10.1097/01.NPR.0000408626.24599.9e avail-able online at *https://www.ncbi.nlm.nih.gov/pmc/articles/PMC5578619/*

11 See "Reactions to Witnessing Ethnic Microaggressions: An Experi-mental Study," Lucas Torres, Alexandra K. Reveles, Felicia Mata-Greve, Sarah Schwartz, and Melanie M. Domenech Rodriguez, *Jour-nal of Social and Clinical Psychology* 39:2, 141-164 (2020), and Keon West, "Testing Hypersensitive Responses: Ethnic Minorities Are Not More Sensitive to Microaggressions, They Just Experience Them More Frequently." *Personality and Social Psychology Bulletin.* 45(11):1619-1632 (2019).

12 Mark Brown, "Michelle Obama tells London school she still has im-postor syndrome," *The Guardian*, 12/3/2018. *https://www.theguardian.com/us-news/2018/dec/03/michelle-obama-tells-london-school-she-still-has-imposter-syndrome*

13 Mark Brown, "Michelle Obama tells London school she still has im-postor syndrome," *The Guardian*, 12/3/2018. *https://www.theguardian.com/us-news/2018/dec/03/michelle-obama-tells-london-school-she-still-has-imposter-syndrome*

14 Martin Luther King, Jr. *Where Do We Go From Here: Chaos or Community,* Beacon Press, ISBN: 9780807000670 (1967).

NOTES

15. "I tell you, my friend, all happiness depends on courage and work. I have had many periods of wretchedness, but with energy, and above all, with illusions, I pulled through them all. That is why I still hope, and hope much." *Honore de Balzac*, letter to friend Laurent-Jan, De-cember 10, 1849, in *The Works of Honore de Balzac, Volume 20*, translated by Katharine Prescott Wormeley (1899).

16. Dorian Lynskey, *How dangerous is Jordan B Peterson, the rightwing professor who 'hit a hornets' nest'?*, The Guardian, February 7, 2018, *https://www.theguardian.com/science/2018/feb/07/how-dangerous-is-jor-dan-b-peterson-the-rightwing-professor-who-hit-a-hornets-nest*; Caitlan Flanagan, *Why the Left Is So Afraid of Jordan Peterson*, The Atlantic, August 9, 2018, *https://www.theatlantic.com/ideas/archive/2018/08/why-the-left-is-so-afraid-of-jordan-peterson/567110/*.

17. Reese Witherspoon, Glamour, Women of the Year 2015, *https://www.glamour.com/story/reese-witherspoon-women-of-the-year-speech* (November 10, 2015).

18. Reese Witherspoon, Glamour, Women of the Year 2015, *https://www.glamour.com/story/reese-witherspoon-women-of-the-year-speech* (November 10, 2015).

19. *Becoming, Michelle Obama*, Crown Publishing (2018), pp. 32.

20. Gallup, *Most Admired Man and Woman*, 2020, *https://news.gallup.com/poll/1678/most-admired-man-woman.aspx*.

21. Kamala Harris, *The Truths We Hold: An American Journey*, Penguin Books (2019), page 18.

22. Kamala Harris, *The Truths We Hold: An American Journey*, Penguin Books (2019), page 17.

23. *National First Ladies Library*, Hillary Clinton, *http://www.firstladies.org/biographies/firstladies.aspx?biography=43* (last viewed 1/5/2021).

24. Please unlearn and relearn about Sacajawea and Pocahontas, if you are relying upon animated movies or children's books. The more accurate telling of their experiences centers their experience and re-veals just how remarkable both were, in the face of threats and vio-lence and racism directed at Native Americans and their families.

25. *Black Lives Matter,* Herstory, *https://blacklivesmatter.com/herstory/* (last viewed 1/5/2021).
26. *See Youth in the Civil Rights Movement, https://www.loc.gov/collections/civil-rights-history-project/articles-and-essays/youth-in-the-civil-rights-movement/,* and *We had Sneakers, They had Guns: The Kids who Fought for Civil Rights in Mississippi,* by Tracy Sugarman, American Folklife Center lecture, 2009-05-05, *https://www.loc.gov/item/2009655474/.*
27. *One of these astronauts may be the first woman on the moon: Eighteen U.S. astronauts have been chosen to train for the Artemis missions, which aim to return humans to the lunar surface, National Geographic,* December 2020, *https://www.nationalgeographic.com/science/2020/12/one-of-these-astronauts-may-be-the-first-woman-on-the-moon/; NASA Outlines Plan for First Woman on Moon by 2024, Paul Rincon, BBC, 9/22/2020, https://www.bbc.com/news/science-environment-54246485.*
28. Krystal Clark, M.Ed., *Equip to Thrive, https://www.krystalnclark.com/workshops.*

About the Author

Cara Tuttle Bell

Cara Tuttle Bell is an award-winning feminist activist-educator who has worked in higher education for over 15 years. Cara holds a Juris Doctor degree from Vanderbilt University Law School, Master of Arts in Women's and Gender Studies from the University of Louisville, and Bachelor of Science in Political Science from Ball State University, where she graduated summa cum laude. She currently serves as the Director of the Project Safe Center for Sexual Misconduct Prevention and Response at Vanderbilt University, where she also is a Senior Lecturer in the College of Arts and Science, teaching in the Women's and Gender Studies Program. Cara is a frequent speaker and workshop facilitator for skills and theories related to women's empowerment.

Cara lives in Nashville, Tennessee, with her husband Lance and dogs Leo and Potus. She is available for seminars, retreats, and speaking engagements based upon her book. Contact her at *cara@drowningintimidity.com*.